Manifold Destiny

The One! The Only! Guide to Cooking on Your Car Engine!

REVISED AND UPDATED

Chris Maynard and Bill Scheller

SIMON & SCHUSTER PAPERBACKS

New York • London • Toronto • Sydney

Simon & Schuster Paperbacks
A Division of Simon & Schuster, Inc.
1230 Avenue of the Americas
New York, NY 10020

First Simon & Schuster trade paperback edition November 2008

SIMON & SCHUSTER PAPERBACKS and colophon
are registered trademarks of Simon & Schuster, Inc.

For information about special discounts for bulk purchases,
please contact Simon & Schuster Special Sales at
1-800-456-6798 or business@simonandschuster.com.

Designed by Dana Sloan
All interior photographs by Chris Maynard

Manufactured in the United States of America

1   3   5   7   9   10   8   6   4   2

Library of Congress Cataloging-in-Publication Data

Maynard, Chris.
Manifold destiny : the one! the only! guide to cooking on your car engine! /
Chris Maynard and Bill Scheller. — Rev. and updated.
p.   cm.
1. Cookery—Humor.   2. Outdoor cookery.   3. Automobiles—Motors.
I. Scheller, William.   II. Title.
TX652.M335   2008
641.5'8—dc22   2008038997

ISBN-13: 978-1-4165-9623-3
ISBN-10:   1-4165-9623-2

Previous editions of this work were published by Villard Books,
a division of Random House, Inc., in 1989 and 1998.

AS ALWAYS, FOR PLUGGY AND MOLLY

Contents

Manifold Destiny

1

In Which We Get Started, and Ask the Question "Why Bother?"

How many of the literary events of 1989 do you remember? How about blockbuster culinary trends? Automotive milestones?

If you can come up with only one answer in each category—and if they're all the same answer—you're no doubt thinking about *Manifold Destiny*, and you're the reason we've turned up again. Not the only reason: we're also back because we're appalled by the exorbitant prices the two earlier editions of *MD* command on the Internet, a realm that didn't even exist (except in Al Gore's imagination) when we first put a pork tenderloin under the hood of a Lincoln Town Car. We could, of course, dribble our own supplies of the book out onto the auction and used-and-rare-book Web sites; as retirement plans go, it beats working for a major airline.

But a new generation of readers deserves the right to learn the pleasures of car-engine cooking without spending more than the price of four gallons of gas. And that very issue—the inflationary spiral that's put unleaded regular in a price bracket with luxury items such as milk—is yet another reason why the world still needs *Manifold Destiny.* What better way to get every penny of value out of the pump than to make gasoline do two things at once? And think of how much less guilty you'll feel about your automotive contribution to global warming if, to use a lousy metaphor, you're planting two feet at once in the same carbon footprint.

A lot has happened in the car and food worlds since *MD* debuted back in '89. The hulking Town Car, which we porkily referred to above, seems positively demure by comparison to any of a flotilla of SUVs that have since lumbered down the pike. And as those behemoths have come under attack, new species of automobiles— the equivalent of the primitive little furry mammals that dodged the dinosaurs—have turned up on the highways. Hybrids are all the rage, and even some hybrid SUVs—the automotive version of furry dinosaurs, to stretch the analogy—are now galumphing across the landscape, promising wonderful gas mileage if you use them only in the city, where you don't need them in the first place.

Eating, as well as driving, has changed a lot in the past twenty years. Thanks to television channels devoted to nothing but food, we now have celebrity chefs, most of whom cook things that celebrity nutritionists tell us we shouldn't eat, thus feeding America's greatest appetite—its appetite for guilt (don't look at us; we did our best to put a whoopee cushion on guilt's stiff-backed chair with *The Bad for You Cookbook*). We've seen vegetarians turbocharge themselves into vegans, vegans take the next step into raw-foodism, and we've followed (at a respectable distance) the emergence of culinary fads such as deconstruction and molecular gastronomy (in simplest terms, the first consists of plating out B, L, and T instead of a BLT; and the second involves turning things into gelatins and foams when they were perfectly fine in their natural states).

Over the past two decades, we've ridden the *MD* phenomenon to such heights of fame that it's a wonder paparazzi don't hang around our doorsteps, waiting for us to throw drunken tantrums or forget to use our seat belts. We've been profiled in *The New Yorker*; made a guest appearance on a live German variety show where we cooked shrimp on the engine of a '56 Caddy while driving around with the mayor of Dortmund and the Caddy's owner, a German Elvis impersonator; fed Eggs-On Cheese Pie (see recipe, page 61) to Katie Couric and Al Roker on the *Today* show (Al went on his diet right after that); bounced a package of veal scaloppine onto the West Side Highway while doing an interview for CBS News; got excerpted in the Library of America's anthology *American Food Writing*; and made it to the top of an Internet list of the ten weirdest cookbooks ever, beating out volumes devoted to roadkill, bugs, poison, ketchup, and cooking in the nude.

And to think that it all started in Schwartz's, on Boulevard Saint-Laurent in Montreal.

Schwartz's is a little storefront delicatessen that cures and smokes its own beef briskets, which it heaps high in the front window partly for display and partly so the countermen can quickly spear and slice them. "Smoked meat" is what Montrealers call this apotheosis of pastrami, and Schwartz's makes the best. You can eat it in the store. You can take it out and eat it at home. Or you may have to eat it on the sidewalk half a block away when the aroma coming through the butcher paper drives you nuts. What we had in mind, one summer's day in 1984, was to pack some in the car for a rest-stop picnic on our way back to Boston.

We were barely out of Montreal when we started to talk about what a shame it was that our pound of Schwartz's wouldn't be so alluringly hot when we pulled over for lunch. When you order this stuff the way Montreal insiders do—"easy on the lean"—room temperature just doesn't do it justice.

It was then that the idea hit. One of us remembered stories we used to hear thirty years ago about lonely truckers cooking hot dogs and beans on their engines. Why not Schwartz's smoked meat? It wouldn't even be cooking it—Schwartz had already done that—but just borrowing a little heat from the engine to warm it up. So we decided, what the hell; if it worked for teamsters, why not us?

We pulled off the interstate in Burlington, Vermont, bought a roll of aluminum foil, and triple-wrapped the sliced brisket. Opening the hood, we spied a nice little spot under the air filter of the '84 VW Rabbit we were driving, which seemed the perfect place to tuck in the package, and off we went. An hour later, we arrived at a standard-issue Vermont highway rest stop, the kind that looks like they wash the trees, and voilà—in minutes we were putting away hot smoked-meat sandwiches that actually had steam rising off them. Best of all, we nearly made two women at the next picnic table choke on their sprouts when they saw that instead of a busted fan belt, we had just dragged our lunch from the Rabbit's greasy maw.

Necessity, to rewrite the old chestnut, is the mother of necessary inventions—like ways to heat smoked meat when you don't have a steam table handy. But since inspired foolishness is the *real* hallmark of civilization, it wasn't long before we were inventing necessities. For instance, a dire need to roast a pork tenderloin on I-95 between Philadelphia and Providence. Car engines, we discovered, are good for a lot more than simply heating things up.

Soon we were calling each other with news of our latest accomplishments:

"I poached a fillet of sole."

"I roasted a stuffed eggplant."

"I figured out how to do game hens."

"I made stuffed wieners."

Before long, those rest-stop stares of disbelief had been replaced by reactions infinitely more delightful to savor—like that of the toll collector who swore she smelled garlic but couldn't figure out where the hell it was coming from.

What we didn't realize, during those early years of random ex-perimentation, was that our burgeoning skills as car-engine cooks were going to serve us splendidly as we competed in one of the most grueling sporting events on the planet: the 1988 Cannonball One Lap of America rally. The One Lap was an eight-thousand-plus-mile highway marathon—seven days of nonstop driving in which participants had to adhere to strict rules while reeking of spilled cof-fee and unchanged underwear. It might have been the most exhaust-ing and disorienting event anyone ever paid money to enter, but it made you feel like a kid with nothing to do except ride his bike in the park for a week—with no grown-ups around. It was so much fun, in fact, that the grown-ups eventually took over. The current version is a lot more serious, involving time trials at actual racetracks, and the entrants—who still have to drive back and forth across the coun-try in eight days—now have to be either pro racers or graduates of driving schools. Back in '88, they'd let anybody in, which accounted for us.

It was damned difficult to stick to the rally routes and get any-thing decent to eat. Most of our fellow competitors followed a regi-men of truck-stop breakfasts (not necessarily eaten at breakfast time) and assorted pack-along calories drawn from the canned and bottled food groups. Our wonderful epiphany, shared by none of the other fifty-seven teams in the event, was that if we cooked on the big V8 under the hood of our sponsor's stretched Lincoln Town Car, we could eat like epicures without screwing up our time and distance factors.

Here's what we did. Two days before the rally started in Detroit, we worked out a menu and did our shopping. Then we comman-deered the kitchen of our friend Marty Kohn, a feature writer for the *Detroit Free Press*, and put together enough uncooked entrées to last us at least all the way to our midway layover in Los Angeles. Boneless chicken breasts with prosciutto and provolone, fillet of flounder, a whole pork tenderloin, a ham steak (a reversion to our simple heat-through days)—everything was seasoned, stuffed, and splashed according to our own recipes, sealed up tightly in three layers of aluminum foil, and promptly frozen. We felt like we were turning Marty's kitchen into a tiny suburban version of those factories where they made airplane food, back when airplanes still had food.

The next day, we transferred our frosty little aluminum packages to the kitchen freezer at the Westin Hotel in the Renaissance Center (try pulling a request like *that* on the next concierge you meet) and had them brought up with our coffee and croissants on the morning of the rally. The food went into a cooler, the cooler went into our Lincoln, and we went into round-the-clock driving mode. Every afternoon between Detroit and the West Coast we'd haul out another dinner, throw it on the engine, and cook it as we lopped a few hundred more miles off the route. Let our competitors use the drive-throughs at McDonald's. We ate well, very well indeed.

We would have done the same thing in L.A. for the return trip, but we didn't have the time. Anyway, it occurred to us somewhere around Albuquerque that we *couldn't* have done it, since none of the people we knew in L.A. had freezers. Everyone there eats out all the time, subsisting entirely on selections from the focaccia, baby field greens, and roasted-garlic food groups.

By the time the rally ended, we'd gained more fame for our means of sustenance than for our position in the final standings: everybody, it seemed, had something to say about car-engine cooking. Half the comments were expressions of pure disbelief, while the rest amounted to variations on "Truck drivers have been doing that for years." This has always annoyed the hell out of us. All the truck drivers we've ever heard of who cook on their diesels are still punching vent holes in cans of Dinty Moore stew.

This is not to say we refuse to acknowledge the pioneers. We are by no means the first people to cook food on car engines. The idea dates back so far, in fact, that it predates cars altogether.

The Huns of the fourth and fifth centuries lived on horseback, and subsisted to a great extent on meat. When a Hun wanted to enjoy a hunk of unsmoked brisket—say, when he was tearing around in the One Lap of the Western Roman Empire (with points for pillage)—he would take the meat and put it under his saddlecloth, and the friction between Hun and horse would have a tenderizing and warming effect. (We think they used saddlecloths. If not, well, just don't think about it.) Since this was a situation in which a "cooking" effect was achieved by the application of excess heat generated by the means of propulsion, it is clearly part of the line of descent that led to hot lunch buckets in the cabs of steam locomotives, and to stuffed chicken breasts à la Lincoln Town Car. We can't say for sure, but it may also have been the origin of steak tartare. In any event, it *did* give rise to the expression "I'm home, Hun, what's for dinner?"

But let's get back to that important qualification—*excess heat generated by the means of propulsion*. This disqualifies a lot of other attempts at mobile cookery, or at least relegates them to a different branch of evolution. We once read, for instance, that the big, handsomely outfitted carriage Napoleon Bonaparte used during his military campaigns was equipped with an oil lantern mounted above and behind the rear seat that could be used for cooking as well as lighting. But whether or not the little corporal used his lantern to heat up leftover veal Marengo, the fact is that lanterns don't make carriages go.

What Napoleon was really onto here was the ancestor of the dashboard microwave, which was being touted as the next big thing when *Manifold Destiny* first came out but which has, mercifully, never quite caught on. Instead, the in-dash space that might have been spewing out popcorn has been occupied by a GPS map gizmo, the greatest inducement to inattention since the cell phone. Plus, sometimes they're not all that bright. We recently heard of a guy who, when it was pointed out to him that he was driving the wrong way on a one-way street, said, "But my GPS told me to take this turn!" Of course, you could skip the GPS and install a DVD viewer, like the one the kids zone out in front of when they're in the back-seat, instead of looking out the window at the Great Smoky Mountains or pissing each other off. They're illegal up front, of course, but tell that to the guy who got the fantods in Miami traffic while his cabdriver watched an in-dash boxing match. But we digress. Suffice it to say that Napoleon wasn't cooking with horsepower.

Car-engine cooking is a lot safer than reading map screens or watching dashboard TV. Since you can't check to see if your dinner is done without getting out of the vehicle and looking under the hood, it's no more dangerous than pulling over to change a tire—a lot less dangerous, in fact, since you don't get to pick the location for a flat tire.

Cooking on your engine is more than just another way to multi-task. Ultimately, it's all about getting some decent chow. Unless you're carrying with you the collected works of Calvin Trillin or Jane and Michael Stern, and have the time to detour to all the wonderful diners and rib joints they have chronicled, a long car trip is likely to bring you up short in the eats department. And it's not like the good old days were any better. We recently came across Henry Miller's book *The Air-Conditioned Nightmare*, based on a six-month cross-country trip he took in a '32 Buick back in 1941. Miller finished the trip in Los Angeles, not only dyspeptic over the philistines and materialists he claimed to have encountered all over the republic, but with his innards devastated from eating in one greasy spoon after another. Poor devil—that '32 Buick had an overhead valve straight eight, as choice a cooking device as any six-burner restaurant range. If only he'd known. And being Henry Miller, he'd probably have felt better about America if only he'd known that in little more than a decade after his 1941 road trip, the philistines and materialists at Rambler were going to produce a car with a backseat that folded into a bed.

But again we digress. The point is that you can make better meals for yourself, on your engine, than the vast majority of the roadside joints can make for you. Not to mention that engine cooking is a great way to sample regional foods. Think about crayfish in Louisiana (see page 94). Lake perch in Wisconsin. Italian sausage in New Jersey. And think of the fun you could have on vacation, with the whole family salivating over that dinner cooking right under your hood. Instead of "When are we going to get there?" the kids will ask, "When will the chicken be done?" Ultimately, the car-engine chef is using one of the tastiest and most healthful cooking methods, simmering foods in their own juices in a sealed package. That's what all the cutting-edge young chefs are doing with their trendy new *sous-vide* plastic-bag-in-hot-water cooking gimmick—only you'll be doing it in foil on the open road.

So now who's the cutting-edge chef?

2

Beginner's Luck—and Skills

A half hour in traffic proves that any dolt can drive, but your first experiences in the kitchen no doubt convinced you that it takes at least a marginally able dolt to make dinner.

While we'll assume that you pass muster on that score, there are nevertheless a trunkful of tips and techniques peculiar to car-engine cooking that you must understand before you start dribbling chicken fat down the side of your exhaust manifold, or down your chin on the side of the road.

HERE'S YOUR ENGINE

Like everything else, car engines used to be a lot simpler. There was a straightforward, uncluttered engine block, with a valve cover either on top or off to one side. A carburetor and intake manifold got the fuel-air mixture into the engine, and an exhaust manifold branched to each of the cylinders to carry off the hot, spent gases of combustion. All the other components—distributor, starter, fuel pump, radiator, fan, and so forth—stood out plain and simple. In fact, the single most plentiful thing under your old hood was air. If you were working on your engine in those days and dropped a wrench, it fell through and landed on the ground.

Today, the ground is one thing you *won't* see when you look under the hood. What with power assists for braking and steering, air-conditioning, fuel injection, turbocharging, emission controls, and other electronic paraphernalia, today's engine compartment looks like an unkempt spare-parts drawer at NASA. As far as things like comfort, safety, fuel savings, and pollution abatement go, this is all to the good. But the cluttering of engine compartments with gadgetry has posed a challenge for the cook.

It's frustrating as hell now to think you know the perfect spot for a package of chicken thighs, only to find it's already taken by the vacuum-assisted pressure sensor for the snibulator pump. We remember reading a story in a car magazine in which a guy described his father's early-fifties technique of securing cans of baked beans to his manifold with baling wire. Aside from the fact that the whole purpose of this book is to take you beyond beans, we defy anyone to find two spots on a modern car engine from which a length of baling wire could be safely secured. For that matter, we defy you to find baling wire, unless your kitchen-on-wheels was manufactured by John Deere.

But there's a positive side to this tangle of technology. Inadvertently, it often affords small crannies in which food packages can be wedged tightly (some of the crannies are especially small, which ties in with the current "portions for one" trend), as well as miles of wiring and tubing that can be used to hold food in place.

But let's throw it into reverse for a second. Despite all these changes—and the fact that many engines are now mounted transverse (sideways) so they can link directly with the transaxle for front-wheel drive—the basic automotive power plant still shares certain fundamental design features with its clean-lined forebears.

Engines, for instance, are still defined by the number of cylinders they have: in the vast majority of cases, four, six, or eight. Volvo and Audi have made fives; Mercedes, BMW, and Jaguar have twelves; the Dodge Viper and some of your beefier pickup trucks have tens. Back in the thirties, Caddy offered a V16; find one of those, and you're set for a whole Thanksgiving dinner. (Get your hands on a two-cylinder Nano—see page 134—or an old three-cylinder Chevy Sprint, and you can roast a couple of chestnuts to have with your Madeira after dessert.) But in most cases, you're looking at four-, six-, or eight-cylinder engines. All of them burn fuel in those cylinders—hence the term *internal combustion*—and, in the process, all of them get hot.

Ah, but how hot is hot, and what parts get hottest? The first thing we should point out is that we're not talking about "engine temperature" as it is expressed by the idiot light, or, if you're lucky, the gauge on your dashboard. Strictly speaking, the dash indicator is giving you the temperature not of the engine but of the coolant circulating between the radiator and the block. When the engine is running properly—in other words, when you're not standing on the shoulder of the Garden State Parkway on a hot July afternoon with your hood up and rubbery-smelling steam pouring out into the pure New Jersey air—that temperature is probably in the low to mid 200s.

No, we're not talking coolant temperature. What we're interested in is the actual temperature of the exposed metal parts of the engine, surfaces that can be a hell of a lot hotter than the coolant circulating beneath them. We've heard the figure 600 degrees Fahrenheit bandied about (and are willing to believe it as far as the exhaust manifold is concerned), but for our purposes, we don't care as much about numbers as we do about results. If you want to play Mr. Wizard, you could buy a couple of those high-temperature thermometers that people stick on their woodstoves and stovepipes (to tell them when to adjust the dampers), and affix them to different surfaces on your engine. We never bother with this, because (a) it is too troublesome and scientific (our dampers are maladjusted too), and (b) on a modern engine, surfaces are so broken up that your foil-wrapped food is likely to be in contact with several components at once. What we favor is the time-tested temperature verification method known as "burn your finger." This is simple. Just get your engine up to operating temperature, turn off the ignition, lift the hood, and touch metallic things with your finger until you burn it. Not third-degree, just the kind of quick hit where you pull your hand back fast and stick your finger in your mouth. Forget trying this on any parts made of plastic—there's a lot of it under the hood nowadays—because it will never get hot enough to do anything more than mildly warm things.

Remember, you aren't necessarily looking for the hottest spots. Car-engine cooking is an extremely inexact science, and there is plenty of opportunity to balance fast cooking on a very hot surface with slow cooking on a not-so-hot surface.

Successful engine cooking comes down to these two questions: How far are you driving? And when do you expect to be hungry?

Besides, cooking temperature is just one consideration. You're looking for a place that's not only hot enough but also commodious and secure enough. We'd much rather take an hour longer to cook a package of stuffed eggplant in a large enough cranny that isn't roaring hot than to jam it into the seventh circle of hell and run the risk of having the foil break or, worse yet, the whole package fall out onto the road. (You try to retrieve an eggplant in traffic, we're not responsible.)

An inexact science, to be sure. We'd love to be able to tell you what location will cook each dish the best on each and every car engine, but the vast number of differences in engines and related components, and in the cooking requirements of various foods, make this impossible. What we can do is offer the accompanying

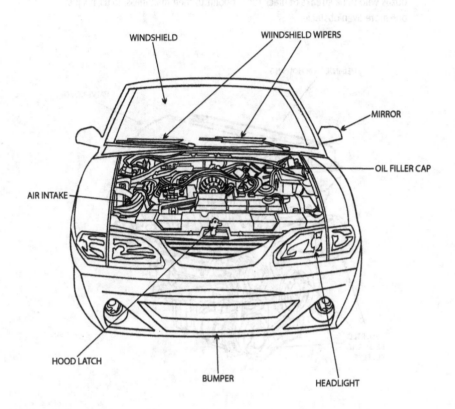

WINDSHIELD

WIINDSHIELD WIPERS

MIRROR

OIL FILLER CAP

AIR INTAKE

HOOD LATCH

BUMPER

HEADLIGHT

IT'S NOT MOM'S KITCHEN, BUT . . .

Some car fanciers seem to be awestruck by the sight of a big V8 nesting in a sea of
tubes and hoses. From a culinary point of view, cooking on one of these is like trying
to do a seating arrangement in the Collyer brothers' house. Just remember, all those
doodads are there for a reason. Whether it's good or bad, don't move them if they
don't want to go.

HOT AS IN HOTPOINT

Turbocharging, as on this Chrysler four-cylinder model, is a popular method of squeaking enough power out of a small engine to satisfy both the EPA and those bozos who think streaks of black rubber point to their manliness. To us, it's just one more oven obstacle.

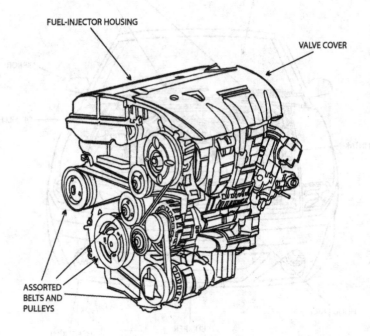

FUEL-INJECTOR HOUSING

VALVE COVER

ASSORTED
BELTS AND
PULLEYS

SMALL ENOUGH FOR A STUDIO

Here's a neat little apartment-size model four-cylinder engine. The fluted valve cover on top will put nice sear lines on your steaks; with a little ingenuity, you should be able to fix a couple of fish fillets on the slanted exhaust manifold guard.

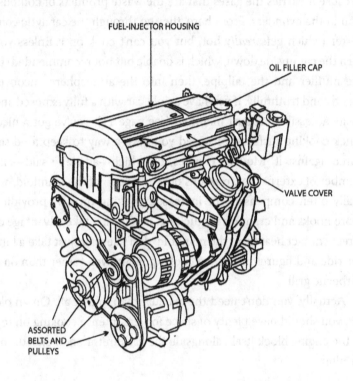

FUEL-INJECTOR HOUSING

OIL FILLER CAP

VALVE COVER

ASSORTED
BELTS AND
PULLEYS

diagrams on basic engine configuration and throw in a few tips on different engine parts. Read up, then roll up your sleeves and resort to the empirical method.

You've probably noticed that we talk a lot about exhaust manifolds. As we said before, this is the hottest part of the engine surface because it carries the gases that are the waste products of combustion in the cylinders. From here, they go through the catalytic converter (which gets *really* hot, but you can't cook on it unless you turn the car upside down, which is doable but not recommended) to the muffler and the tailpipe, then into the atmosphere, inconveniently and truthfully. If you have an old car with a fully exposed and easily accessible exhaust manifold (see page 11), you've got a nice, quick cooking surface—provided you have a way to keep food secured against it. Modern engines, on which—as we've said—any number of external contraptions obscure much of the manifold, actually often compensate for increased cooking time by providing more nooks and crannies for tucking. If you can't take advantage of direct contact heat from the manifold, don't despair; just take a longer ride and figure that you're cooking in an oven rather than on a barbecue grill.

Actually, you don't need the exhaust manifold at all. On an old V8, you should have plenty of space for less intense cooking on top of the engine block itself, alongside the carburetor and beneath the air filter.

NOTE: When exploring the possibilities of this territory, *never* put anything where it will interfere with the free movement of the accelerator linkage. This will not be a problem on some newer top-of-the-line models, where the mechanical linkage has been replaced by an electronic throttle control. Also, *never* think you can use the air-filter housing as a warming oven, no matter how much empty space there seems to be in there.

Even smaller cars have their engine-top possibilities—remember, that historic first package of Schwartz's smoked meat was wedged alongside the air filter of a four-cylinder diesel Rabbit.

The best setup we have ever come across for easy access, top-of-the-engine cooking is the upper surface of the in-line six in a 1965 Jaguar XKE. If you can think of no other reason to own an E-type Jag—in which case your soul is as dead as a road-killed armadillo—consider that long, uncluttered block, the top of which is formed into a deep *V* by the slanted valve covers on either side. The plugs come in right at the top, but they hardly interfere. This is the place for roasting elongated items like pork tenderloin or eye of the round. What's more, the cooking area is so nicely exposed that you never even have to get grease on your bony, aristocratic knuckles where they poke through the holes on your driving gloves. Until Subaru comes out with an optional teppanyaki grill, the Jag gets our convenience award.

FIVE NO-NOS

1. Interfering with free movement of the accelerator linkage. This is a spring-loaded device (other than on cars with electronic throttle control; see page 18) that connects the gas pedal with the carburetor or fuel-injection system, thus regulating the flow of gas to the cylinders. If it jams, either you won't go or you won't stop. *Give it a wide berth.*
2. Blocking the flow of air into the engine's air intake. Internal combustion requires gas and air. *Let your motor breathe.*
3. Indiscriminate yanking on wires, hoses, and so forth to secure food packages. Better you eat at a burger joint than pull out a spark-plug wire. *If the package doesn't fit, don't force it.*
4. Placing, checking, or removing food with the motor running.

CHRIS MAYNARD AND BILL SCHELLER

Being a fan belt means never having to say you're sorry. *Come back with the same number of fingers you started with.*

5. Foil-wrapping foods with too much liquid. Aluminum foil may make a wonderful customized cooking vessel, but a pot it's not. *No car owner's manual calls for basting the engine.*

Spark plugs can actually be as much of a help as a hindrance. When you find them set into a recess deep enough to require an extension on your socket wrench at tune-up time, you've also found a good spot to insert small, individual items like boned chicken thighs. If the plug recesses are close to the exhaust manifold on one side of the engine, the food placed there will cook faster, so, depending on the recipe, stop along the way and move your packages from one side to the other. Otherwise, you could be embarrassed—as we once were—by baked apples baked only halfway across. (We haven't baked apples since, but feel free to give them a try.)

Fuel injection, now standard on all makes, presents some interesting possibilities. Look under the hood of a late-model car and you'll often see a shiny flat surface, usually made of cast aluminum, that sits right up top on the middle of the engine. That's the housing for the fuel-injection apparatus. While there are often little niches beneath which you can jam things between the housing and the engine block, what we're really interested in is that griddlelike expanse up top. We first tried it in the Lincoln Town Car we drove in the One Lap of America rally, and we were disappointed to find that it was good only for warming precooked things like cured ham steak with a side of baked beans. That shouldn't have surprised us, since the fuel injectors are pretty far removed from the fiery innards of the engine. But we reasoned that since a good deal of ambient heat is trapped under the hood, and the housing is made of a conductive material, it was worth another try.

Our faith in the injector housing was vindicated on a drive along the Maine seashore in an '88 Chrysler New Yorker with famous food writer Alan Richman, who was doing a piece on us for *People* magazine. Eager to impress Alan, we stuffed and partially boned a couple of Rock Cornish game hens, wrapped them into nice flat little packages, and gave that smooth aluminum surface another try. After two hours of driving, we opened one package and discovered that the birds were not only cooking but browning beautifully. We flipped the packages over, got back on the road, and ate the little hens, done to a turn, after only four hours of touring the scenic Maine coast.

So, it all depends on the car.

We have to offer two caveats regarding fuel-injector-housing cookery—or, for that matter, cooking on any flat surface you find atop your engine. The first involves hood clearance—the gap between cooking surface and hood. If there's too much clearance, your food is going to fall off. And if there isn't enough, you're going to slam the hood down and squash the packages, break the foil, and make a mess. We were lucky with the game hens—they flattened just enough, rather like a pressed galantine; this probably helped them cook as well as they did. The same tight fit might enable you to make panini, the Italian sandwich rage of the moment . . . and also enable you to brag to your friends that you have a $28,000 panini press.

So here's the strategy. Before you put any food on the injector housing, make a cone of aluminum foil about four or five inches high. Put it on the housing and shut the hood. Now lift the hood and see how much of the cone has been flattened. Too much? You'll have to cook flat food, like fish fillets. Not very? Then wad some additional foil and place it atop your packages of food to hold them in place. It's that simple.

The other caveat has to do with the weather. When it's really cold outside—say, less than 20 degrees Fahrenheit—the moderate heat that you get atop the injector housing usually won't do the trick. We

AN OLD PRO TURNS ON HIS STOVE

An experienced engine chef lovingly places dinner atop a fuel-injector housing. He's already done the foil-cone test (see page 21) and knows the hood will keep it secure. He also knows enough to keep his bare fingers away from the hot metal.

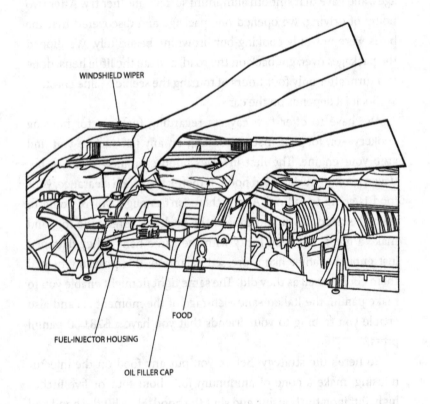

WINDSHIELD WIPER

FOOD

FUEL-INJECTOR HOUSING

OIL FILLER CAP

A SMALL PORTION FOR A SMALL DIET

If you've got a small appetite (we don't) and can make do with small portions, there are some bite-sized places on the engine available for cooking. Here, our chef wedges an appetizer between the valve cover and the oil dipstick. Wedgies like this are best removed slowly and carefully.

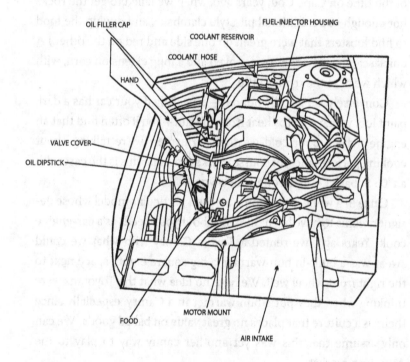

OIL FILLER CAP

FUEL-INJECTOR HOUSING

COOLANT RESERVOIR

COOLANT HOSE

HAND

VALVE COVER

OIL DIPSTICK

MOTOR MOUNT

FOOD

AIR INTAKE

remember the time we had to do a car-cooking demonstration at a winter street fair in the tony Hudson Valley town of Piermont, New York. The pièce de résistance was stuffed boneless chicken breasts, done atop the injectors on a Pontiac Grand Prix—but it was so damned cold that day that even though we'd driven all the way up from Paterson, New Jersey, the chicken wasn't done. (It reminded us of the time on Cape Cod, years ago, when we failed to get the rocks hot enough in a traditional pit-style clambake, and dug up the food to find lobsters that were green on one side and red on the other.) A quick search led us to a toaster oven and a long extension cord, with which we bent the truth a little.

Conversely, on a really hot day—especially if your car has a dark paint job, which absorbs heat from the sun—you'll often find that an engine that's a poor cold-weather performer (we're talking about cooking performance, of course) perks right up. This is the case with an '05 Subaru Outback one of us owns.

Once in a while, you'll come across a particular model whose designer seems to have been thinking about your needs as a car-engine cook. Years ago, we rented a Toyota Camry with what we could swear was a built-in bun warmer, a big square empty space next to the right front wheel well. We have no idea what the Toyotans were thinking when they put a bun warmer in a Camry, especially since theirs is a culture that places no great value on baked goods. We can only assume that this was yet another canny way to play to the American market.

A COOK'S COMPARISON: SIX LATE-MODEL CAR ENGINES

Every now and then, we saunter into showrooms and pester those eager, wide-eyed folks who stand around hoping against hope that you are not only going to order the SX, LE, Limited Edition model of whatever they're selling but are intent on ordering the sun roof, the moon roof, the Halley's Comet roof, the premium interior lighting group, the forty-speaker DVD entertainment system, and the silicon bronze lug nuts. We tell them who we are, wait for the squeals and gasps of excited recognition that never come, and politely ask if they'll pop hoods so we can poke around engine compartments and make notes on just what kind of cooking surfaces we're looking at. They seldom object—after all, they don't have much else to do.

You can't cook on 'em all—not without running up a hell of a rental car bill—but after a while, experts like us know what to look for. We can usually tell whether we're sizing up the rolling equivalent of a six-burner Viking or a Kmart hot plate.

Car makers, of late, have made our job a little more challenging. Some of them seem determined to design engines that look like sleek little modular pods with as few irregular surfaces as possible. All of them are replacing whatever metal surfaces they can with plastic, especially in the form of sheathing over our beloved, griddle-like fuel-injector housings. (One salesman recently told us that the plastic "has better damping qualities," whatever that means, and that cast aluminum tends to rust, which it doesn't. It does tend to pit slightly, but that can be prevented by using olive oil as a preservative.) But all these innovations have merely inspired us to become more resourceful in discovering toasty little nooks, crannies, and what we like to call "tuck spots" for our foil packages of dinner.

Here's a rundown on the relative merits of six 2008 models, representative of current trends in four-, six-, and eight-cylinder design, plus a gas-electric hybrid. Remember, we've only scratched the surface. There have been hundreds of engine configurations down through the decades, and each calls to the car cook in its own special way. Experiment!

Make and Model	Engine Type	Comments
Chevrolet Aveo	1.6-liter 4-cylinder	The aluminum manifold cover in front gets nice and hot, but the near-vertical surface makes secure food placement nearly impossible. The top of the engine is covered with a plastic sheath, but a nice nest of hoses to the right of the engine looks promising. There's also space between the engine and air filter on the left, though the lack of intense heat here may make longer cooking times necessary.[1]
Ford Mustang	4.0-liter V6	Two tuck spots appeal to us here. There's one at the right rear (remember, right and left are when you're facing the engine) alongside the injectors, under the oblong box that serves as a terminus for the spark-plug wires. Another spot, on the left between the injector housing and the valve cover, seems to offer space for small packages, maybe an individual fish fillet or boneless chicken breast.[2]
Chrysler Sebring	2.4-liter 4-cylinder	Another car with a big plastic sheath over the engine. One saving grace, if you're more into heating rather than cooking, is the three hot-dog-on-a-bun-sized indentations in the sheath. These would also serve well for something like the packages of smoked meat we brought back from Schwartz's, especially if it's a hot day and the car has a black paint job. Otherwise, nooks and crannies are virtually absent.[3]
Hyundai Tucson[4]	2.7-liter V6	In keeping with the "crossover" principle (i.e., part SUV, part wagon) Hyundai engineers covered only part of the Tucson's engine—the front part—with one of those damned plastic sheaths. To the rear is a nice open aluminum surface with two big recesses that offer the possibility of a partial tuck under the plastic sheath.[5] There are a couple of obscure tuck spots on the right, but they're very deep, with a frustrating tangle of wires above. If you ever do get something wedged in there, you might wind up saying the hell with it, and leave it for whomever buys the car from you.
Ford Edge	3.5-liter V6	There's a promising spot on the left, alongside and slightly beneath the injectors. Also, look for a deep recess toward

Make and Model	Engine Type	Comments
Ford Edge	**3.5-liter V6**	the front, just behind the valve cover. The big question, though, is whether the edgy types that drive this thing in the TV commercials ever stop to eat, or whether they're always too busy heading to the next edgy club in their edgy clothes.
Chevrolet Tahoe Hybrid	**6-liter V8 coupled with an electric motor**	Chevy made only 8,000 of these behemoths in 2008, apparently to prove that it's possible, in the realm of carbon footprints, to cross a ballet slipper with a size 13 Doc Martens.[6] Obviously, the car cook has to approach the cavernous engine compartment from the right, where the gas engine lives, and preferably while standing on a stepladder. It's hard to find a usable metal surface on the plastic-sheathed Vortec V8; the best tuck spot is too close to the belt. But we're intrigued by the possibilities of the gap between the two motors, hidden beneath a nest of bright orange wires.[7]

[1] How much time do you want to spend driving around in a car this small?

[2] We have mixed feelings about six-cylinder Mustangs. We realize that sixes were an option even in '64, when the car was introduced, but it was the 289-cubic-inch eight that caught the attention of high school boys like us. We suspect that six-cylinder Mustang buyers might be raw-food vegans, rendering the question of chicken breast "tuck spots" moot.

[3] The Sebring is the car equivalent of a steam table.

[4] As born-and-raised easterners, we have a problem with a certain automotive naming trend. We've been waiting patiently for a Ford Providence, a Nissan Newark, a Chevy Altoona . . .

[5] Don't let food packages slip under the sheath unless you have a socket wrench handy. Also, the aluminum surface will require the foil-wad security method (see page 21), and it's a long way from there to the underside of the hood. You'll need lots of foil, but, then again, the wads are reusable.

[6] The Tahoe Hybrid is supposed to get 20 miles per gallon in either city or highway driving, which is respectable given the gas-only version's mileage, but the real advantage is the word *Hybrid* in big letters on the side of the vehicle. If you live in a college town, and are worried about getting your paint job ruined by an environmental studies major brandishing the key to his Toyota Yaris, this flashy logo is the protection equivalent of having a "Passaic County Honorary Deputy Sheriff" badge on your car when you're illegally parked in Paterson, New Jersey.

[7] Like other hybrids, the Tahoe has a 110-volt outlet in the passenger compartment. This makes it possible to tote along a hot plate, microwave, espresso machine, or Ronco Showtime rotisserie, totally eliminating the need to rummage around under the hood for tuck spots.

WILL IT SMELL FUNNY?

This is not a particularly bright question, but it is asked so often that we have to address it yet once more. The usual phrasing is "Won't the food smell like oil and gas?" or "Is there any danger from the exhaust?"

Let's put the answer this way. When you check into the Hotel Cipriani in Venice and throw your complimentary terry-cloth bathrobe over the heated towel rack, do you worry about getting it wet? Of course not, because you know the hot water that heats the towels is *inside* the pipes that make up the rack. If it isn't, Cipriani is in big trouble—the same as you are if there's oil and gas sloshing around under your hood outside the proper channels. (If the leak is bad enough to cause serious food contamination, your engine probably won't be running long enough to cook anything anyway.) As for exhaust, it should come out of the pipe at the back of the car. If it is leaking through faulty plumbing anywhere farther up front, it is likely to get into the passenger compartment and enable you to discuss your next meal with Escoffier himself.

Still, the outer surfaces of a car engine are seldom squeaky-clean, and by "blackened," Cajun chefs don't mean tainted with crud from a valve cover. This is why one of the first rules of car-engine cooking is to wrap *everything three times* in aluminum foil. It makes checking for doneness a bit of a pain, but it virtually guarantees a hermetic seal that locks flavor in and dirt out. Remember, *three times*. No more, no less.

FOOD SELECTION AND PRECOOKING PREP WORK

Although the Triple-Foil Wrap rule is the key to successful car-engine cookery, there are a few other dos and don'ts that, when applied with a dose of the plentiful highway commodity called common sense, will assure that things get done properly (or, in cooking terms, properly done).

First, keep your recipes simple. You'll notice that along with regional variety, simplicity was one of the main criteria in our selection of recipes. This is not because we believe, like the Shakers, that it's a gift to be simple; on the contrary, much of what is really fun and worth doing in this world is, like nature itself, idiotically complex. Gilt lilies are the very stuff of life: we once boned a whole capon, stuffed it with alternating layers of chicken mousseline, duxelles, and spinach soufflé, and wrapped it in brioche. But we had the good sense to cook it in an oven, not on a car engine.

One thing to remember is to avoid recipes that involve a lot of liquid, since this will make the foil packages easier to puncture, and messier if that should happen. (The only exceptions to this rule are situations involving cans or semirigid containers, and engines with the sort of flat, secure surfaces that can accommodate them.) Also, you're better off if the foods you wrap can be contoured against hot parts of the engine, preferably with the bulky foil seam on the outside, for better contact and heat distribution. (See below.) Don't use cuts of meat, fish, or poultry that are too thick. And bones, if left in, will make packages too rigid—as well as increase cooking time.

WRAPPING TECHNIQUES AND ALUMINUM FOIL COMPARISONS

We've all wrapped our share of leftovers.

Bundling up meals for engine cooking is a similar procedure, only more precise—like wrapping Christmas presents. First, make sure nothing you're wrapping is going to poke through the foil (chicken-wing tips can do this). If you spot potential trouble, wrap the pointy parts loosely, wadding foil as necessary to provide a cushion in the innermost foil layer; the two outer layers can be wrapped more snugly. Second, leave enough foil on the sides to make a secure, overlapping fold. Bring the foil up around the top of the food and make a flat, interlocking seam, like the ones on a pair of good blue jeans, and tuck the excess underneath on both sides. You might try alternating the direction of the seams (top to bottom) on each successive wrapping, but if all your seamless sides run on top of each other, be sure to put the seamless side of your package against the engine for better heat distribution.

In past editions of *Manifold Destiny*, we didn't recommend heavy-duty foil. We've reconsidered that stance, especially in light of Reynolds's recent introduction of a heavy-duty product with a nonstick surface on one side. As you'll see from our notes accompanying the comparison chart, this is a useful innovation. But there's no need to use the nonstick foil beyond the initial inner wrap; use one layer of regular heavy-duty or two layers of conventional foil for the outer wraps. As for whether to put the shiny or matte-finish side out—not an issue with the nonstick, as you have to have the matte side face the food—we feel it makes no difference. Shiny packages make a nicer display, though, when you're showing off to friends, rest-stop acquaintances, and state police officers you're trying to bribe with a halibut steak.

Last but not least, be careful when unwrapping, since you may want to rewrap to continue cooking. All aluminum foils become brittle when heated, as heat rearranges their molecules to a more orderly pattern. So it's a good idea to buy better-quality foil—and to think about the heavy-duty option.

Here are the results of tests we have performed on four varieties of foil. Except for the Shurfine, all purchases were made in April 2008 in Morrisville, Vermont.

Brand Name	Quantity (in sq. ft.)	Thickness in inches[1]	Price	Structural Integrity (scale of 10)
Price Chopper	75	.0009765[2]	$2.99	8[3]
Shurfine	200	.0009764	?[4]	5
Reynolds Wrap Heavy Duty	50	.0014648	$3.99	10
Reynolds Wrap Release Non-Stick[5]	35	.0014648	$3.99	10

[1] As we do not own expensive digital micrometers, measurement of foil thickness was made by folding a sheet into 128 layers, like mille-feuille pastry, smacking it flat with a meat-tenderizing mallet, measuring with a ruler, and doing the necessary division.

[2] We have a hell of a ruler.

[3] Structural integrity was tested by holding strips of foil between two hands and snapping it, and also by tearing strips lengthwise to determine how straight the tears were.

[4] The Shurfine foil was discovered in the basement of a family home being cleaned out prior to sale. It was probably purchased at the Big Y in Longmeadow, Massachusetts, in 1973 for $.89.

[5] The Reynolds Release brand of nonstick foil was tested against a control product, Reynolds Wrap Heavy Duty conventional foil. The test was performed by tightly wrapping 4 x 4-inch pieces of chicken skin in single-thickness packets of each foil, and subjecting them to twenty minutes in a 400°F toaster oven. The chicken skin wrapped in the Release nonstick foil did in fact release beautifully, with no sticking. The chicken skin wrapped in the conventional foil stuck significantly, requiring the use of a sharp knife for removal. Had the skin been attached to an actual chicken component, unsightly tearing of the skin would have resulted. This problem can of course be avoided by oiling or buttering the inside surface of a conventional foil, as we recommend throughout our recipes. Another excellent lubricant is liquid chicken fat, which can be obtained by heating chicken skin in a 400°F toaster oven for twenty minutes.

There isn't much to be said about food placement that wasn't already covered when we talked about engine configuration. When they designed your car engine, they also designed its available cooking surfaces, and what you see is what you get. Keep in mind, though, that you can compensate for lack of direct heat by increasing cooking time, or for excessive heat by decreasing cooking time.

When you do decide on a surface to use, watch out for sharp protuberances that might puncture your foil wrapping. Little nubs and knurls can be handy, though.

ALL WRAPPED UP

What can we say about wrapping with tinfoil? We can say: Do it neatly, do it tightly, do it thrice.

Step 1: Place food in the center of a sheet of foil.
Step 2: Pulling the foil snugly against your lunch, crimp tightly to make a good seal.
Step 3: Fold the ends toward the center of the package and crimp again.
Step 4: Neaten up by pressing the foil into a snug package with no protruding flaps to catch and tear during cooking.
Step 5: Repeat two more times so the food is securely wrapped in three layers of foil.

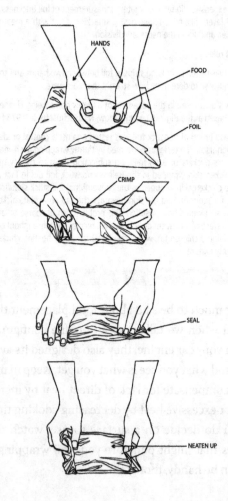

We've had some success with packages wrapped so that excess foil at the ends can be used as tabs to twist around protruding parts, thus holding the food in place. Use what you can find: the oil-dipstick sheath, the narrow tubing associated with the emissions-control system, you name it. Just don't run your tabs across too wide a gap— aluminum foil ain't baling wire.

So much for the mechanical angle. The remainder of what there is to be learned about car-engine cuisine has to do with how food behaves, and with the different modes of cooking and the foods to which they are best suited.

Forget boiling. At first, you might think that a car engine is a great place to boil things, because there's no way you can watch the pot. But think about it: even if you found a hot enough spot on the motor, and a cooking vessel that would fit it, you'd have about as much success boiling something in there as Chrysler did putting record players in the glove compartments of '57 DeSotos. (Don't laugh; they tried it.) You'd leave a trail of soup, even on the smoothest roads.

Likewise, don't think you can roast anything to a crispy stage of doneness—the best you can hope for is a nice browning, as we got with the game hens on the injector housing of the Chrysler New Yorker. This you try to accomplish by minimizing the liquid in your recipe, or keeping it on the engine long enough and in a hot enough spot for the liquid to cook away and leave the surfaces to brown.

What you *can* do nicely is braise foods—cook them gently in a small amount of liquid, just enough to transfer the heat and serve as a vehicle for seasonings. This is where wine comes in handy, as in our recipe for Poached Fish Pontiac (page 108)—but remember to keep that open bottle in the trunk. When you're working with something delicate, like fish fillets or veal, also be sure to rub the inside of your innermost sheet of foil with plenty of butter or oil to prevent sticking (for notes on the new nonstick foil, see the chart on page 31).

Then there's a whole class of apparently simple low-rent dishes that at first glance seem made for car-engine cooking, but that we emphatically do not recommend. We hadn't really thought about grilled cheese, for instance, until we ran across a piece in *The New York Times* about an unnamed "famous and rich performer" who, while traveling the world and staying in swanky hotels, always carries a roll of aluminum foil and a clothes iron. Upon arriving in a city before a performance, she heads for the nearest food store and picks up some cheese and a loaf of bread. She makes cheese sandwiches, wraps them in the foil, and cooks them under the iron in her hotel room.

This goofy maneuver presents a certain dilemma. On the one hand, it's pretty tacky and takes advantage of a free energy source (the hotel's electricity), and on those counts we're in favor of it. But there are two drawbacks. First, the bread and cheese you're likely to pick up at five-thirty on a Sunday afternoon in Moscow, Idaho, probably won't be the kind you'd really want to eat. It would be a lot simpler to just get something like a Stewart Systems Styrofoam-and-cheese concoction and let some sleazy bartender heat it in the micro. After all, your hotel iron probably doesn't serve drafts.

The second drawback is that room service, especially in the best hotels (we're assuming that you're not always traveling through places like Moscow, Idaho), is one of the crowning glories of Western civilization. If you can pick up the phone, press one button, and cause food and drink to magically appear at your door, why bother burning your fingers heating bad cheese and white bread into an indistinguishable, colorless mass under an iron?

Or on your car engine? One of the points in favor of engine cooking is that it allows you to enjoy good food that you've made yourself using good ingredients. If you're just going to start heating and melting, you're only slumming, like Ms. Famous-and-Rich.

At the other end of the spectrum, there are the fad cooking techniques. The Westin Hotel in Calgary, Alberta, for instance, used to flog a new gimmick called "hot-rock cooking." According to the pop-up folder they put on the night table in your room, it was "the latest European restaurant trend—cooking your own food on a hot rock at your table" (the one in the restaurant downstairs, not the one by your bed). Neither of us got to try this silly business on our last pass through Calgary, but it occurred to us that this "latest trend" is really nothing more than a pedestrian version of engine cooking. The big difference is, when you're done cooking on your hot rock, you're still in Calgary, while if you had fixed a nice veal cutlet on your engine, you'd be up in the mountains heading for Lake Louise by the time it was done.

Still, for those of you who can't resist a new craze, we have accommodated the hot-rock idea to car-engine cookery. First, wedge the biggest rock you can up against your exhaust manifold. Drive for about a week to get it hot (depending on the direction you take, you might still be in Alberta if you start out in Calgary). Now stop your car, slap some food on the rock—unwrapped—and wait for the edges to curl.

A word of warning: There's some odd food up in the Canadian home of hot-rock cooking. At the same Westin, the breakfast menu was hawking low-cholesterol artificial eggs for omelets. When asked if the eggs came from artificial chickens, the waitress replied, "No, they're from Dome Petroleum."

FIND THAT ROLLS!

Consider the phantom 1920s Rolls-Royce, a car we heard about from a curbside well-wisher in Manitou Springs, Colorado, when we stopped for lunch during the big rally. This guy was watching us conduct a fuel-injector-housing foil-cone test (while at lunch, plan for dinner), and told us that he had heard of a Jazz Age Rolls that had had a little oven cast right into the engine block. A special touring model, he said it was. Did this wonderful car ever exist? And if it did, was it one of a kind or an extremely limited-production model? Why wouldn't the PR people at Rolls talk with us when we called them? Why, if what they were trying to come up with was a Toyota-style bun warmer, didn't they call this edition a Buns-Royce? Why would they do that, when "Buns-Royce" sounds like a dancer at Chippendales? Why is there being rather than nothingness?

Ask questions. It's the only way you'll learn anything.

TIMING, EQUIPMENT, AND SAFETY

When you set out to learn how to cook the way normal people do, all you have to do is master the ways in which different foods react to different treatments and temperatures—for example, the ability of egg whites to expand and hold air, the tendency of cream sauces containing egg to curdle if you get them too hot, and the fact that you can panfry a steak better in cast iron than in stainless steel painted with a token wash of copper. You don't have to go to the Cordon Bleu to learn these things, but if you do, you can write a serious cookbook renouncing everything you were taught and yammering about how Western cuisine should be influenced by the dietary predilections of the !Kung Bushmen of Namibia.

You don't have to study under a despot in a toque blanche to learn car-engine cooking either, but it will help if you remember that you'll be dealing with the peculiarities not only of different foods but of different engines. Nowhere does this come across more clearly than in the matter of timing. When we suggest times in our recipes, don't take us too seriously—and likewise, don't follow your own recipes chapter and verse when it comes to converting and timing them for use on the old V6. *Experiment*. Something that took us four hours may take you two if you have access to a hotter part of the engine. Or the reverse may be true. About the only general rule we can lay down is that dishes almost always take longer to cook on a car engine than they do on a stove. Like we said, it's an inexact science. Relax and enjoy the scenery.

The downside to learning how to work a particular, beloved automobile engine like a six-burner Viking is that you'll hate like hell to sell the car. The only consolation is that when you run the ad in the paper, you can throw in a come-on phrase such as "Cooks like a champ."

When we first wrote *Manifold Destiny*, we hoped that eventually onboard computers would come to the aid of car chefs. In those days, it looked as if more and more cars were going to be equipped with computers that could tell you the gas mileage you were getting at any given moment and how far you could go on the gas you had. By now, these gizmos could have been set up so you could program them with pertinent data—what you were making and where on the engine you had to put it—and they would tell you how long it was going to take to cook and where, at any given speed, you would be when dinner was done. But the mileage computers never really took off, and if they had, they would be too depressing to look at nowadays. They'd probably be connected to your online banking statement, so you could see how much of your net worth was being siphoned off to OPEC with every mile you drove.

Maybe some offshoot of the OnStar system will do the trick. You know OnStar—it's the satellite link that alerts the Strategic Air Command, or Ernie's Texaco, or somebody, when your airbag goes off. Well, picture it configured so you could give the relevant recipe information to the satellite, then sit back and let the satellite tell you when dinner was ready to eat. (In our Northeast recipes section, page 53, we've got yet another suggestion for the OnStar folks.)

At this point we should address the issue of rareness and doneness, which relates to the latest installment in the "Fear of Food" movement that has sprung up since the first edition of *Manifold Destiny* came out. Like a lot of other reckless souls, we like meat that hasn't been cremated to a uniform shade of gray throughout. (We know, we know . . . the FDA says to cook it gray all the way through.) We should point out that most of the problems with contaminated meat have involved hamburger, which isn't recommended for car-engine cookery anyway (although we like this rare too, preferring to grind our own if it comes down to that). But if it makes you feel any better, just drive farther. Far be it from us to get in the way of the government telling you how to eat.

The equipment requirements for car-engine cooking are minimal. It helps to have an oven mitt or two, though there's nothing wrong with the old gloves you keep under the seat for shoveling snow and changing tires. It would be nice to mount a paper-towel dispenser under your dashboard, and maybe another for aluminum foil—it pays to keep extra foil on hand, so you can rewrap food after you tear the foil when checking to see if it's done. Beyond these basics, there exists the unexplored realm of specialty cooking equipment made only for use on car engines. We'd love to see a pot manufacturer come out with a line of covered vessels made to fit securely in the larger under-hood crevices of popular models—if for no other reason than the sheer pleasure of walking into a kitchen-gadget shop with a name like The Blue Nantucket Turnip and asking for a saucepan to fit an '07 Buick Lucerne. Or maybe auto-parts stores could sell them. Our other dream gadget is a lasagna pan that would slide into special flanges attached to the underside of the hood. (We can't figure out how this would work, though, without dumping tomato sauce onto the windshield wipers.)

A KIT FOR THE CAR KITCHEN

If the Scout motto "Be prepared" remains a guiding principle in your life, you probably have stashed in your trunk a road emergency kit containing car-repair tools, a flashlight, spare fuses, flares, an ice scraper, and so forth. Why not be prepared for impromptu engine cooking as well? You never know when you'll pass a grocery store running a special on boneless chicken breasts.

In addition to an ample supply of aluminum foil and paper towels, here are some essential items with which the rolling kitchen ought to be equipped. Feel free to elaborate or simplify to the extent of your own ambition; what we've listed will see you through most of the recipes in this book.

- Eating utensils and plastic plates. If it won't make your car look ridiculous, carry one of those Edwardian baskets containing a Royal Doulton service for twelve.
- Small cutting board. Plastic is better than wood, since you probably won't be cleaning it right away. Wood retains bacteria if you don't scrub it pronto—that's why all those commercial butcher blocks wound up in trendy antique shops. Even if you do use plastic, wash it after every outing—especially if you've been cutting raw meat.
- A couple of sharp knives. A French chef's knife and a boning knife should cover all situations.
- Mixing bowl, two quarts at the most
- Metal spoon for mixing. Wooden spoons are nice, but they present the same problem as the cutting board (see above).
- Plastic measuring cup
- Pounding mallet. If you get one made out of rubber, you can also use it to knock out minor dents.

- Salt, pepper, and assorted spices: pick out the ones you use most frequently. A plastic squeeze bottle full of cooking oil isn't a bad idea, but we wouldn't want to store it in a hot trunk for too long.
- Rubber gloves for handling the occasional hot pepper, when you can't wash your hands right away.
- Can opener
- Oven mitt(s)

Remember, again, these critical safety tips: *Stay away from the accelerator linkage.* Don't move, remove, or block anything crucial to the car's operation. Always shut the engine off when you put food in to cook, and when you check to see if it's done. Avoid moving parts in general, especially pulleys, belts, and the radiator fan. (Get your fingers near that fan, and your car engine will become a food processor rather than a stove.)

PRACTICE RUNS: A COUPLE OF EASY FOOD CATEGORIES THAT WILL BREAK YOU IN AS A CAR-ENGINE COOK

For all our disparagement of the heat-a-can school of car-engine cookery, we nevertheless remember our roots at Schwartz's and also recognize that some timid souls will be looking for a way to ease into this wonderful new technology. Here, then, are a few tips on what we call the "ready-made" and "ready-bought" categories of food.

Around 1920, the Dadaist artist Marcel Duchamp shook up the world of aesthetics by attaching manufactured items such as snow shovels and porcelain urinals to gallery walls and calling the result art. Ready-made art, to be precise. Nowadays, the giant food-processing companies, using supermarkets as their galleries, have

taken a page out of Duchamp's book and offered us a vast array of
ready-made food. It's manufactured, to be sure, and it can inspire
the same sort of arguments as the stuff Duchamp put on display.
Was that art? Is this food?

For better or worse, it's possible to pull off the highway into a supermarket lot anywhere in America and come out with something
marginally resembling dinner—just heat on your engine and serve.
The basic choices can be found in either the canned-goods or
frozen-food section. These suggestions are presented only for rank
beginners and those in dire need of a car-cooked food fix; they involve about as much creative thought as trying to figure out whether
to turn right into the Taco Bell or left into Denny's.

Canned goods fall into two categories—liquid-packed, and semi-
solid mush. The first group includes such items as green beans,
baby peas, Irish potatoes, and stewed tomatoes. The second takes in
such crowd-pleasers as corned-beef hash, baked beans, and dog
food. For the automotive chef, the cooking methods are the same
for either category. Remove the label, punch a couple of small vent
holes in the lid, cover lightly with a square of foil, and find a place—
preferably on or close to the manifold—that allows as much direct
contact with the can as possible. If simple wedging will not secure
the can, perhaps shims of crumpled foil with help. (If you insist on
being a classicist, try baling or picture-hanging wire.) The liquid-
packed items will cook somewhat faster; if you overcook any of
these, they'll be even mushier than usual. If you overdo something
like hash, you'll get some crustiness around the edges, but this might
actually improve the texture. At any rate, make sure the cans are securely in place and drive until steam comes out of the vents—maybe
forty-five minutes to an hour for the average fifteen-ounce can.

**Do not, under any circumstances, try this procedure with-
out punching the vent holes.** Without them, a can could explode
under your hood. Even if it doesn't, you could still be in a lot of
trouble. Just as the temperature of your antifreeze can rise above

its boiling point because the system is sealed, so can an unvented cartridge of SpaghettiOs get a lot hotter than 212 degrees Fahrenheit. Remember the whooshing fountain you got last time you popped the cap on an overheated radiator before letting it cool? Imagine that fountain being full of superheated, sticky pasta, which will stick to you, and tin-can shards, which will stick *into* you. We can give pretty close to a money-back guarantee this is what you'll get if you don't vent cans before heating. *Be warned!*

On the foolproof side, but showing no more imagination, are frozen foods. Just pick out your favorite, and shove it under the hood. Heating will take considerably less time if you defrost foods first, though this is best done in the refrigerator to prevent spoilage. Even with that, you may run into problems with sogginess when you predefrost. Not for nothing do the packages tell you, "Do not thaw before cooking." In any event, try to use some common sense: a small frozen loaf of garlic bread covers the business zone of most car engines a lot better than a twelve-inch frozen pizza. If you're using old-fashioned frozen food, the aluminum packaging may already be in place (e.g., TV dinners); just wrap in an outer layer of foil and you're all set. If it's packaged for the microwave, rewrap it entirely in foil. For obvious reasons, boiling bags are not recommended, although the elusive foil pouches (we still haven't found them at our local supermarkets) might hold some promise if you triple them, as we've recommended on page 32).

Obvious suggestions (virtually everything about frozen food is obvious) include shoving enchiladas or fish fillets between fuel-injection intake ports and jamming a Swiss-steak dinner on top of a manifold. Just remember that less-than-solid foods slip and slide. Try to cook a pizza vertically and you'll wind up with a dough disk rising majestically from a swamp of tomato puree and mozzarella. However, frozen peas loosely wrapped can be made to fit just about anywhere. Cooking times will range from about thirty minutes for loose vegetables to two hours or more for some of the beefier entrées.

Ready-boughts is a subject much closer to our hearts. The big difference between ready-mades and ready-boughts is individuality, and the intensity of the maker's intent. A good automotive analogy might be the difference between a so-called Indy Pace Car and a low-rider bopping down the bad end of Sunset Boulevard. Detroit pounds out a limited number of Pace Cars; the number is limited by how many saps will shell out several grand extra for the lettering on the side. (The first time we saw a "Pace Car," we almost believed it. Then we thought, "What's it doing on Route 9 in Worcester, Massachusetts?")

IF YOU INSIST ON COOKING READY-MADES . . .

As you may have gathered, we are not terribly enthusiastic about cooking off-the-shelf or "ready-made" foods on car engines. For one thing, they're too easy: how can you derive any sense of accomplishment from merely raising the temperature of something that's already been cooked in an industrial vat in Camden, New Jersey? For another, the realm of ready-mades has been getting shabbier and shabbier of late. Once there were just canned foods and frozen vegetables, but over the past couple of decades, the TV dinner crossbred with the microwave oven and strange new creatures were hatched. Supermarkets now devote entire freezers to bizarre vegetable-pasta-cheese-sauce concoctions that can be either boiled in the bag or zapped in the micro, and "pocket" meals based on pita bread, croissants, and turnover dough. The vast majority of these things are designed to be microwaved while they're still frozen, and many are not suitable for the gentle heating a car engine offers even if you do take them out of their plastic bags, defrost partially or completely (see page 42), and foil-wrap them. But if you must cook the already cooked, there are a few standbys that always do well under the hood. Here are our choices:

- Hot dogs, knockwurst, kielbasa, and the whole family of pre-cooked sausage products you'll find in the shrink-wrap section of your supermarket meat cooler. These have the advantage of cooking fast, and of being dispersible throughout the engine compartment should conditions so dictate. Best of all, they can be mixed and matched with two of the basic food groups . . .

- Sauerkraut and baked beans! In popular folklore, canned beans are usually depicted as the original car-cooked food. As we've mentioned, though, finding room for cans in today's engine-compartment environment is a chancy business. (B&M's seven-ounce size opens up the most possibilities.) The modern way to cook beans in transit is to empty a can into a foil packet, starting with a double thickness of foil to prevent tearing when you bring the sides up for wrapping. You can pop in a few frankfurters or other sausages (see our Bohnen Mit Wurst recipe, page 127), whole or in chunks, and customize the package to fit about anywhere—just be careful of sharp objects. The same goes for kraut. Either cook it separately, transferred from a plastic bag or can into foil, or make up a choucroute garnie that includes your favorite precooked pork products. Just drive until it's all heated through, usually an hour at most.

- Spam, and its cousins in the world of monosyllabic meat products. Spam has lost its allure for many of us who once loved it in the campfire days of childhood, long (for us) before it acquired its nefarious new meaning, but it does have the advantage of heating quickly, either whole (an engine Spam roast) or in individually wrapped slices tucked against the engine hot spots for that fried effect. Just plork it out of the can and onto the foil.

- Corned-beef hash. As malleable as baked beans but not as prone to leakage, hash is at its car-cooked best when you spread it into a flat foil package and do it up brown atop an injector housing that gets fairly hot. Foil-wedge for security, and turn once for uniform crisping. Now, if only you could poach an egg somehow . . .
- Little canned hams. Back in the fifties, we thought these were the only things they made behind the Iron Curtain besides atom bombs. These Polish exports are still on the shelves, often in sizes small enough for engine cooking. As with Spam, all you have to do is de-can, foil-wrap either whole or in slices, and slip onto the old mill.

A low-rider, on the other hand, is one of a kind. Someone makes it for himself, not particularly caring that BMW owners will chuckle at it condescendingly or that every third cop will pull him over if business is slow that day. One person decides how high the lifts will go, how purple the flocking will be. *He* decides how many dice will hang from the mirror, how many pictures of his mother will be painted on the doors. It's his car, and tough nuts to the rest of the world.

Food is the same way. Stouffer's makes its stuffed chicken breasts according to a recipe calculated to offend the fewest number of potential eaters. Oregano? Too spicy for Minneapolis. Real provolone? Too ethnic for Memphis. Thyme? No, someone in Phoenix might realize that it doesn't take that much time to do it yourself. It's like the Indy Pace Car: make it seem distinctive, but keep it palatable to as many people as possible.

Now put those glaciated chicken breasts aside, and step into

Tony's Delicatessen on 204th Street in the Bronx. (You can tell you're in the presence of an original, as Tony is an Italian running a traditionally Jewish business in a heavily Irish neighborhood.) Walk up to the display case and gaze at the potato logs. They're cylinders of mashed potatoes, rolled in bread crumbs and deep-fried. Next to the logs, in keeping with the axle-and-wheel motif, are corned-beef *doughnuts*! These are made of finely ground corned beef, pressed into doughnut shapes, crumbed, and also deep-fried.

Why on earth would anyone make doughnuts out of corned beef? They're heavy as hell, and oily enough to require an EPA variance on the Arctic tundra. On the other hand, why not? Tony makes them and Tony likes them and that's good enough for Tony. Financially, it's a little better for Tony if you buy a few, but he doesn't really care. You're already in the deli, so you'll probably buy something. Who cares if it's a corned-beef doughnut or a meatball hero? Not Tony. Tony would like low-riders if he lived in east L.A.

Ready-boughts make for a marriage of two American ideals, freedom of choice and automobiles, and they are a natural for novice car-engine cooks. You could hop in your car and eat Tony's corned-beef doughnuts straight from the store, of course, but your hands would get so greasy that you'd lose control of your car on the Hutchinson River Parkway. The answer? Wrap 'em in foil, stick 'em on the manifold, and stop at the Mobil station near Mamaroneck to chow down. Just bring plenty of napkins.

A FEW OF OUR FAVORITE READY-BOUGHTS

The beauty of ready-boughts is that you never know when you're going to find them. They aren't advertised, they aren't mass-produced and delivered frozen to the point of sale, and you'll never find them on the menu at franchise joints. They're out there, waiting to be discovered, in shops that anchor neighborhoods you probably wouldn't be driving through if you weren't hungry for something special.

- **Smoked pork chops.** In or around any metropolitan area with a good-sized German population, you'll find shops generically known as "pork stores," in which Mr. Pig makes his leap at immortality. Among all those homemade sausages you'll likely find *kassler rippchen,* pork chops cut from a smoked loin. These are a great way to have your chop and eat it without a long engine-cooking time—the smoking has done the work, and all you have to do is heat them through.
- **Noodle kugel.** Find a Jewish deli that cooks up big lasagna-sized pans of this dish, which was invented to determine whether noodles could be used as a construction material. Its noodle base is baked with sour cream, cottage cheese, raisins, and sugar (we did see a simplified "light" kugel recipe once, but we filed it with romantic heavy metal and cheerful Bergman movies under *O* for *Oxymoron*). Just have the counterman quarry off a slab, then heat.
- **Deviled crabs.** The Hampton, a Virginia restaurant, is nothing more than two house trailers stuck together, located about a block from where the excursion boats leave for tours of the Atlantic fleet's mooring in Norfolk. Hampton may not have a lot to offer besides easy parking and cheap crabs, but what more do you need? Pick up a couple, rewrap in foil (keep the crabs in their little aluminum pans for form and crispness), and let 'em roast.
- **Cornish pasties.** These delicacies from the Upper Peninsula of Michigan may be a precursor of the idea of boil-in-a-bag meals, except you get to eat the bag. A hefty lunch of cubed meat, potatoes, and vegetables packed into a crescent (not a *croissant*) of stiff dough, it's perfect for munching while you're looking for

grasshoppers in Nick Adams's dreamfields along the Big Two-Hearted River.

- **Coiled bologna.** (Not to be confused with the ignition coil.) Gallon jars filled with a tight coil of sausage look like a page out of *Gray's Anatomy.* They're handy because you can cut chunks customized to fit the nooks and crannies of your engine.
- **Stuffed peppers.** Cruise the backwater towns of north Jersey until you find an Italian deli that stuffs its own peppers. You're looking for a bread stuffing heavy on the oil and garlic, something with the mean density of plutonium. The beauty of these is that you can drive from Paterson to Atlantic City with a couple of them on the engine and they won't get soggy. How could they? If they're made right, they already are soggy.

Ready-boughts are the forgotten flip side of the regional-cuisine trend, and places like Tony's and Schwartz's have their counterparts everywhere. In Kentucky, many small taverns serve rolled oysters—behemoth bivalves rolled and stuffed with cracker crumbs to the point of being a large bulge of cracker moistened with essence of oyster. In Essex, Massachusetts, Woodman's—which lays serious claim to being the inventor of the fried clam—sells clam fritters, balls of deep-fried dough studded with chunks of chopped clam. Going to Buffalo? Pass up the chicken wings and stop for some beef on weck, thinly sliced beef sandwiched into a sweetish caraway-seed roll. The list goes on and on: deviled crabs in Newport News, molded onto a thin piece of aluminum that will create a nice crusty bottom when it heats up. Coiled bologna (see sidebar, above) is a North Carolina specialty. Whenever you get peckish, just heat up about eight inches and keep driving. And don't forget the inspiration for *Manifold Destiny*—smoked meat cut from the brisket at

Schwartz's or any of the lesser lights among Montreal's delicatessens. All of these delightful ready-boughts are out there waiting to be wrapped in foil and savored on the road. There may never be a Northwest Passage, but there are still a lot of things in America worth discovering.

3

Car-Engine Recipes: American Regional Cuisines

The car-cooking craze (if we may modestly call it that) and the popularity of American regional cuisine came in at just about the same time. "American regional," of course, can mean a lot of things. At one end, it's a celebration of wild edibles that can be harvested/caught/shot only in certain locales, or of dishes linked to ethnic groups that happened to settle here, and not there. At the other end, it's McDonald's selling lobster rolls in their New England franchises.

At its best, the trend has sparked a revival of the dishes your mother used to make, if her family had lived in the same place for two hundred years—assuming, of course, that she was a decent cook to begin with. It can also be a celebration of spectacularly unspectacular cookery, as we're reminded every time Garrison Keillor uses "hamburger hot dish" as a laugh line at his fellow midwesterners' expense.

We've arranged our recipes geographically, using a formula that also brings in, wherever possible, the car culture and highway ambience of four sections of the United States. And with a nod to our neighbors on this shrinking globe, we conclude with a selection of international recipes.

A few words about cooking times: In the recipes that follow, we precede the ingredient list with a recommended mileage figure. Keeping in mind what we said earlier about time being a far more important factor than distance in car-engine cooking, we hasten to point out that our recipe mileage numbers are based upon an average speed of 55 miles per hour. Thus, a 110-mile recipe will take two hours to cook. We know that you can do 65 legally on most stretches of interstate, and that you, personally, will probably go faster, but you may get slowed down by something along the way, like a rest stop or a cop. Conversely, if you're stuck somewhere like the Santa Monica Freeway or Route 46 in Clifton, New Jersey, you'll cover a lot less mileage before dinner is ready.

Finally, a note about storage before cooking. If you're leaving on a four-hour trip and you're planning to cook a two-hour dish, you'll want to keep your prewrapped food cool until it's time to put it on the engine. Unless it's wintertime and you're using your trunk as a fridge, bring a small cooler to keep perishables from spoiling in transit. If you have a really long haul ahead of you, you may even want to freeze meals in advance, as we did on the rally. Attempt this only if you have a properly insulated cooler and plenty of ice—and cook your meals immediately after thawing to prevent spoilage. We're not responsible for food poisoning due to improper refrigeration; consult a comprehensive cookbook or home-economics manual for the details of freezing and thawing.

THE NORTHEAST

The Northeast is where American cookery was born, on the massive hearths of our Colonial forebears. Well, someone's Colonial forebears. Between the two of us, we have only one of a possible four sets of grandparental forebears who ever cooked over a Colonial hearth. The rest of them, back in those distant days, tended hearths in places like Quebec, Switzerland, and the hinterlands east of Naples. We had a good laugh over one of the sillier dicta to come down recently from the Olympian earnest foodie heights, namely, "Don't eat anything your great-grandmother wouldn't have recognized as food." This would leave out an awful lot of things Mr. Earnest Foodie must approve of; in the case of one great-grandmother, whom we knew personally prior to her untimely death at 101, it would have included just about anything that didn't come from the macaroni food group.

Those Colonial New England hearths did give rise to a wonderful cod-and-cornmeal-based cookery, but the true great gift of the Northeast is its ethnic repertoire—particularly that superb cuisine brought to our shores by the above-mentioned great-grandmother. She and her kind have been followed by a vast and varied array of immigrants, recipes in hand. In Paterson, New Jersey, where one of us grew up back when the city had only one Chinese restaurant (it served only two dishes, and you know what they were), there are now Turkish restaurants, Peruvian restaurants, Ecuadorian restaurants . . . places representing each of the dozens of ethnic groups that showed up over the past forty years. Our theory is that no one told them that the silk mills had shut down, so they figured they'd all make a buck by feeding one another. They do not, however, "fuse" their food; you can't walk along upper Main Street and find a joint run by some clever chef who decided to offer the world Turkish-Ecuadorian cuisine. The Turks and Ecuadorians alike would boycott the guy, and he would have to move his business to New York City.

There, people who are neither Turkish nor Ecuadorian, and whose idea of really clever fusion is Morgan and Stanley, would think the idea was the greatest thing since soy sauce met maple syrup.

Farther north, New England—a place founded on rigorous religious principle—is making more food news than at any time since the days of the Colonial hearth. It's the spiritual home of people who care deeply about what they eat, and where it comes from. These are the folks behind the "locavore" movement.

What are locavores? They're people who try to eat only foodstuffs grown within close proximity—usually one hundred miles—of where they live. When you think about it, New England is a funny place to get excited over an idea like this, since its growing season lasts roughly from the Fourth of July to Bastille Day. Back when everyone was a locavore out of sheer necessity, it was perfectly plausible for folks to swallow a famous newspaper hoax about a town in Vermont where they froze the old people in the winter so they

wouldn't have to feed them. The population of New England locavores, needless to say, tends to swell in the summer.

Nevertheless, there persists a hard-core intent on spreading the locavore gospel, saving on food-delivery mileage by ruining the lives of all the hardworking souls who produce lemons, olive oil, wine, chestnuts, chocolate, Scotch, marmalade, filberts, Parmigiano Reggiano cheese . . . you get the idea. One of the leaders of the movement is New England environmentalist Bill McKibben, who bravely champions this agriculturally challenged region's ability to eke out the essentials for the hundred-mile diet. But maybe he's onto something—maybe he's got a formula for a mixture of barley, root vegetables, Cheddar cheese, and maple sugar that he'll dry, crumble up, and sell under the brand name "McKibble."

Us, we're going to go be locavores in southern Italy.

So-Be Subie Spinach Paks

Vermont, where one of us lives, is the home of the most loyal Subaru owners in the nation. Vermonters like Subarus because they have all-wheel drive, which is the only way they can get from one place to another (i.e., from their houses to their mailboxes) for six months of the year. The cars are also a big hit in Vermont because they have opposed-piston engines, and Vermonters are opposed to just about everything.

In gratitude, Subaru christened its most popular model in the state's honor. This is the Outback, named for the universal answer to the question of where anything is on a Vermont homestead, as in:

"Where's the dog?"

"Out back."

"Where's the rototiller?"

"Out back."

"Where's that transmission I took out of the old Subaru?"

"Out back."

Vermont is also home base for the "artisinal" movement in food, a close relative of the "locavore" movement. It's easy to be an artisinal locavore in Vermont, since there's an artisan making artisinal cheese, artisinal bread, and, for all we know, artisinal Ring-Dings within two gallons of gas of any location in the state. They even raise artisinal chickens in Vermont.

So, hop in your Subie and go collecting. Snag some artisinal vegetables, some artisinal goat cheese, and some artisinal eggs from one of those chickens, and slap together a nice snack to hold you over on the way back from the recycling depot. Never mind that this dish originated with the South Beach diet; with the right ingredients, you can exorcise all that Floridian frivolity and make it at home in Puritan New England, where we're all sinners in the hands of an angry

God . . . especially when we drive all the way to New Hampshire to save money on top-shelf gin.

DISTANCE: 40–50 MILES

> 1 pound locally grown organic spinach (last time we looked, it was only $8 a pound at the Saturday farmers market in Burlington), heavy stalks removed
> 1/2 locally grown organic sweet red pepper, minced
> 1/2 small locally grown organic onion, minced
> 2 ounces artisinal goat cheese, cut into small dice
> 2 free-range eggs, beaten
> Salt and pepper to taste. Tell your friends it came from the salt and pepper mines in South Tunbridge; what the hell do they know?
> Butter for greasing foil

Steam the spinach on your woodstove until wilted; press out the moisture and chop (chop more wood while you're at it). Mix with the other ingredients, then plop into the center of a piece of buttered (and you know what kind of butter) foil. Do the two outer wraps carefully, so you can reuse the foil. Find a reasonably hot spot on your engine, and don't drive too far from home.

Hyundai Halibut with Fennel

New England fishermen used to call big halibut "doormats." For this recipe, get your steaks cut from one that looks more like a floor mat. If you have a Hyundai Accent, use MSG for seasoning.

DISTANCE: 55–85 MILES

4 halibut steaks (or fewer, with other ingredients reduced
    proportionately, if you are short on engine surfaces)
Butter for greasing foil
1 teaspoon oregano
Grated rind of 2 lemons
1 clove garlic, minced
2 fennel bulbs, thinly sliced
Dry vermouth or dry white wine

1. At home or on the road, lay the halibut steaks on 4 pieces of buttered foil. Sprinkle with the oregano, lemon rind, and garlic. Add a generous layer of fennel slices and sprinkle with vermouth or wine. Wrap tightly.

2. Cook 1 to 1½ hours, depending on the thickness of the steaks and the cooking location.

V8 Venison Cutlets

Years ago, when life was simpler and so were computers, talking cars were limited to the Saturday-morning cartoons. Auto communication was limited to a horn and turn signals that told the next guy when you were turning into his path.

Then things got more complicated, and plans arose for cars that told us via little beeps that we were drifting toward the brick wall along the parkway. Then vehicles appeared that, through the same beeps, told the brick wall it was about to be creamed.

Now we can get systems that, after we hit that brick wall, promptly tell the proper authorities who we are, when we hit the wall, and precisely where that wall is (or was, depending on your speed and mass). Help is on its way, and you don't even have to find your cell phone. As you lie panting in pain, still strapped into your statusmobile, you can rest assured that help, of one sort or another, is on the way.

As in the rest of life, there may be unforeseen consequences. One particularly delicious one might be along the Merritt Parkway in Connecticut's Fairfield County, one of the richest in America. There, lush estate plantings have jumped the deerproof fences and spread along the roadside, with good and bad news for the local deer population. Living becomes easy, with the table always set for company, but it also becomes deadly, as the rush for a seat collides with expensive automobiles, also rushing, with their seats full of local swells.

Sadly, *Odocoileus virginianus* loses every time, but it's not all for naught. In Connecticut, dead meat on the road belongs to the driver that killed it, a state of ownership easily transferable. According to the General Statutes of Connecticut, the original "wounded deer act" of 1937 required that a vehicle be "legally operated upon the public highway" before the owner and/or operator took ownership of the remains. In a perhaps unspoken commentary on the circumstances of many of these collisions, the "legally operated" part was dropped in 1949.

Now, in the absence of the operator, or if said operator doesn't want to take a few pounds of bloody Bambi back to his McMansion on the hill, the authority in charge can give it to whomever wants it, first come, first served. Which is where the loudmouthed computers take over.

"Squack, squarracckk! Exit thirty-three, northbound, Den Road, small doe, 'bout ninety-five pounds, well fleshed, no open wounds, what am I bid?"

"Skkrreech frakkchichi! At exit forty-two, Weston Road, I got an eight-pointer, look terrific over the fireplace in that new great room, goes about 225, what'll ya give me?"

Welcome to America's first market-driven, computer-facilitated meat exchange. Locales like Fairfield County exist because of the Holy Market, and now they can simultaneously keep it tidy and feed off it. Think of the cyber-call-for-help as a spotting scope, outfit your servants with loden green breeches and lots of paper towels, and have them serve you in your driveway.

DISTANCE: 30–50 MILES

Per serving:

    2 thin venison loin cutlets
    1 teaspoon finely minced garlic
    $1/2$ teaspoon dried rosemary
    Salt and pepper to taste
    Butter for greasing foil

1. Pound the cutlets very lightly, then dust with garlic and rosemary. Add salt and pepper to taste.

2. Wrap snugly, with the innermost of your three foil layers well buttered.

3. Try to place along fairly smooth parts of the engine block or

exhaust manifold to promote even cooking. If the meat is thin enough, turning will not be required.

NOTE: If rabbits are the only animals crossing the parkway, cook as above, bearing in mind that it takes many more to make a meal. That's why bunnies breed so insistently.

Eggs-On Cheese Pie

*T*his recipe, which originated in a medieval monastery, was our star turn on the *Today* show a few years back. It works best on cars with a large horizontal cooking surface that gets fairly hot. It also involves the use of some auxiliary equipment, i.e., washed-out tuna or cat-food cans. These are handy items, by the way, to include in your road-kitchen kit.

You can scale the recipe up or down depending on how much of a cooking surface you have.

DISTANCE: 55 MILES

Butter for greasing cans
Bread crumbs
4 ounces mozzarella, diced
3 eggs
Salt and pepper to taste

1. At home or on the road, butter the insides of 3 clean tuna cans. Toss a couple of tablespoons of bread crumbs into each can, shake to distribute, and dump out the excess. Cover the bottom of the cans with about half of the diced mozzarella, then break an egg into each can. Add salt and pepper, then cover with the remaining mozzarella.

2. Tightly wrap each can in foil so there will be no spilling, and set on your flat engine surface.

3. Cook about 1 hour, or until the cheese is melted and the eggs are set.

NOTE: Make sure you do the foil-cone test for hood clearance, as outlined on page 21, before you try this recipe. If the cone smashes down to a height exactly the same as the cans, you're in luck—the insulation pad under the hood will hold them in place for you. If the space is smaller than the cans, give up. Think what a damned fool you'll look like with tuna cans outlined in bas-relief on your hood. If the space is larger, use our foil-wad security system (see page 21). But put the foil wads *under* the cans, rather than over them, because the cans will be soft on top.

Suburban Scalloped Scallops

Years ago, certain well-off groups found it necessary to cruise around in vehicles big enough to carry a year's provisions, not because they had to but because lesser mortals couldn't. Two early models were International Harvester's Travelall and Chevrolet's Carryall; the '50s weren't big on exploring language.

These gigantic arks were often handed down through families where parents were referred to as "Father" and "Mother" or perhaps "Poppy" and "Mater." (It was also the beginning of the odd WASP custom of giving boys' names to defenseless little girls.) Until 1961 the Travelall had only three doors, and the Carryall waited until 1972 for its fourth.

But that was fine, because they were used mainly to haul the paraphernalia of horse people: oiled saddles and Hermès riding boots, redolent of old hay and manure. Sugar cubes and broken whips gathered dust in the corners of the vast cargo area.

The nonequine families tended to use them as station cars, assuming that the local train stopped at the Atlantic Ocean. Here the load tended to be kids, blond, of course, in sun-bleached bathing suits, and collections of cracked beach pails dating back more than twenty years. In later years, fiberglass shards from surfboards would appear as the youngsters became old enough to drive.

One thing these modern-day covered wagons never seemed to carry was food. We assume that such basics were delivered by whatever small markets offered charge accounts; the cook or housekeeper doubtless called in orders a week at a time. Gin, whiskey, and cheap wine were probably stocked at the beginning of each summer, when large trucks had an easier time on the local roads.

Times have changed. The Travelall disappeared in 1975, perhaps a victim, on the consumer side at least, of smaller spreads and fewer shared family experiences. Chevy, however, adopted the attitude of "looking tough is as good as actually being tough" and took up its alternate name, Suburban, full-time. It registered the title as a trademark in 1988, and the rest is history, way too much of it. Back in the heyday of Mustang and Cougar, we would have called it the Whale.

An obvious choice for dinner in these parts is seafood, perhaps scallops, which are native to the chilly New England waters, cook easily, and go well with potatoes. Get the large sea scallops if the local market carries them; failing that, try to purchase . . . oh, what the heck, just tell the cook you want scallops, because she's going to be doing all the work anyway.

DISTANCE: 30–45 MILES, DEPENDING ON HOW FAST THE COOK DRIVES

Per serving:

  2 large sea scallops, roughly 3 inches in diameter
  Butter for greasing foil
  Splash of dry vermouth (that green bottle next to the Gordon's)
  3 tablespoons heavy cream
  Pinch of tarragon
  Salt and pepper to taste

1. Slice each scallop in half longitudinally, like an English muffin (even Father will be able to do this). Arrange on well-buttered foil, two pieces per packet. Sprinkle with vermouth, then cream, then seasonings.

2. Wrap in smooth foil packages, and place as close to the exhaust manifold as possible. On an older model there will be enough room to fit several good-sized goats under the hood; ask Cook to use her imagination. Drive until the scallops are heated through, which is pretty much the same as being cooked through. It doesn't take much.

Of course, if you're a true WASP, the odds are you won't know the difference anyway. Chow down, and don't forget the cloth napkins.

Pat's Provolone Porsche Potatoes

As opposed to the couch variety.

DISTANCE: 55 MILES

½ pound new potatoes
1 cup milk
1 cup water
Butter for greasing foil
2 ounces aged provolone, grated

At home, peel the potatoes and slice them about ¼ inch thick. Place in a saucepan with the milk and water and simmer about 10 minutes. Drain and spread on heavily buttered foil—the number of packages you make is up to you, depending on the characteristics of your engine. We recommend at least two, for optimum heat distribution. Sprinkle the potatoes with the grated provolone and dot with butter, then wrap. Cook about 1 hour.

Thruway Thighs

*T*here's a New England tradition of stuffing turkey with oyster dressing, especially at Thanksgiving. This struck us as odd when we first heard about it, since, despite having similar IQs, oysters and turkeys come from such different backgrounds. But, then again, so do scallops and bacon.

In order to streamline the turkey-and-oyster-dressing concept, we came up with a version that mates the marvelous mollusk with quicker-to-cook boneless chicken thighs. This was the pièce de résistance, along with Cornish game hens, on that memorable 1988 drive up the Maine coast with Alan Richman (see page 21), back when *People* magazine, for whom Alan was chronicling our exploits, still covered high culture rather than devoting itself exclusively to drunken teenage starlets and their quests for intellectual parity with poultry and oysters. It was Alan, in fact, who came up with the charming alliterative name of this recipe.

DISTANCE: 50–200 MILES, DEPENDING ON THE CAR (SEE BELOW)

NOTE: Cut all ingredients in half if you are short on cooking surfaces.

    2 medium or 3 small leeks, white parts only, thinly sliced
    1 fennel bulb, with stalks, thinly sliced
    4 tablespoons (¹/₂ stick) butter, plus extra for greasing foil
    ¹/₂ cup chicken broth
    1 dozen oysters, shucked, the liquor retained (or buy shucked fresh or
        frozen oysters)
    8 chicken thighs, boned and butterflied
    Salt and pepper to taste

1. At home, gently sauté the leeks and fennel in 2 tablespoons of the butter, then braise in the chicken broth until soft. Drain, reserv-

ing the broth. Meanwhile, sauté the oysters in the remaining butter until the edges curl. Thoroughly combine the leeks, fennel, and oysters (break up the oysters, which will help you distribute them better), moistening with the reserved chicken broth or oyster liquor, or both, if necessary. Stir in salt and pepper.

2. Lay the chicken thighs on individual pieces of buttered foil. Distribute the stuffing mixture among the thighs, folding one-half of each thigh over the other half and wrapping tightly.

This delicious dish nicely illustrates the variations in cooking times among different engines. The first time we tried it, we were driving a 1988 Chrysler New Yorker, and it took three hours and forty-five minutes to cook the thighs to perfection. The second time, an Olds Cutlass did the job in only fifty minutes. The big difference was that on the Chrysler, we placed the thighs in and around the fuel-injector ports. On the Olds, they went straight onto an unusually accessible exhaust manifold. Cars being what they are today, figure on the longer side for cooking time—but if you're driving the Maine coast, there'll be plenty of places to stop for fried clams while you're waiting for the main course to be done.

You won't be in *People* magazine, unless you're famous and get stopped by a Maine state trooper for driving and eating clams with a baby in your lap.

Impressive Veal Impreza

"Impreza" is another one of those goofy names the Japanese come up with for perfectly good cars, which, if Americans had thought them up, would have been christened after fierce animals, or maybe scenic locales out West. The Germans would have named them after sports, like polo or golf, while the Chinese would have taken an already-existing Detroit name and replaced one of the consonants, as they recently did with their "Chery." As China looms larger as an automotive colossus, we expect to see showrooms full of Forgs, Nuicks, and Podges—but no, these won't be in showrooms at all. They'll be in the car aisle at Wal-Mart.

Anyway, we imagine that the boys upstairs at Subaru got their first look at the engineering department's latest offering one day, and one of them turned to another and said, "Nice car, Masayoshi. I'm really imprezed with it."

"Me too, Katsuro. Let's call it the Tribeca."

DISTANCE: 30–50 MILES

Per serving:

4 ounces veal cutlets, pounded and cut into strips
4 ounces asparagus, cut into 1-inch lengths
2 tablespoons olive oil
1 small clove garlic, mashed or finely minced
1 teaspoon lemon juice
Salt and pepper to taste

At home, toss all the ingredients together and let marinate for 30 minutes. Wrap, making separate packages for separate servings. Make sure the veal and asparagus are distributed in each package so that they come in equal contact with a hot part of the engine. If the engine contact point is only mildly hot, turn once during cooking.

Down the Shore Cavatelli, Sausage, and Broccoli Rabe

People in New Jersey don't go to the shore; they go "down the shore." And when they get there, they eat Italian food. You can stroll down the boardwalk in Seaside Heights and have a *zeppole* (sugared fried dough) for a morning snack with your coffee, stop at a sausage-and-pepper or pizza stand for lunch, and head a block inland to any one of dozens of Italian restaurants for dinner. The Jersey Shore is so imbued with the tradition of Italian eateries that proprietors change their names to sound Italian—we found a restaurant called Duffinetti's, started by a guy named Duffy, and a bagel shop (probably run by an Eddie Cohen) called Bageleddi's. There are sub shops at the shore that sell scungilli (sea snails, sort of like conch) and big plates of escarole and beans. It's that Italian.

This recipe was inspired by a dish we enjoyed at a restaurant in Lavalette. You've got to pronounce the ingredients right—cavatelli, little rolls of pasta dough that are shaped somewhat like gnocchi, are pronounced "cavadeel." Broccoli rabe, sold in some supermarkets as "rapini," looks like nature's test run for broccoli, more stalk than florets and unusually bitter, for a vegetable. It's pronounced "broccoli rab." Now you sound like a New Jerseyan of southern Italian ancestry, and not like some professor from Milan.

Make this while you're heading down the Garden State Parkway on a Friday night, in the middle of July.

DISTANCE: 70 MILES (LESS IF THE TRAFFIC ON THE PARKWAY IS BAD)

2 cups cavatelli, cooked al dente at home
1/4 bunch broccoli rabe, blanched and coarsely chopped at home
2 links Italian sausage, hot or sweet, thinly sliced
3 tablespoons grated Parmesan
2 tablespoons olive oil

(continued)

3 tablespoons dry white wine
1 to 2 cloves garlic, finely chopped
Dash of red pepper flakes
Salt and pepper to taste

At home, toss all the ingredients in a bowl. Heap onto foil and wrap. The dish is done when the sausage is no longer pink, and the motel in front of you is.

Safe-at-Any-Speed Stuffed Eggplant

When we introduced this dish, we noted the play on Ralph Nader's book *Unsafe at Any Speed*, and said of our eggplant offering that "unlike the Corvair, if you handle it right, you don't have to turn it over." We decided to keep the recipe in this edition, because we like eggplant—but we have to note that (a) Ralph Nader is no longer funny (and we doubt he thinks we ever were), and (b) one of us once owned a Corvair, which was a nice little car that never, ever turned over on us.

We're leaving this recipe in the Northeast section, where it was originally placed because of its ethnic flavor ("Like Ralph Nader," we wrote, "this dish has a Middle Eastern pedigree"). We resisted the temptation to move it to Florida and rename it "Electoral Eggplant Hash."

DISTANCE: 165–220 MILES

1 medium eggplant (about 1 pound)
¾ pound ground lamb
2 tablespoons olive oil
1 medium onion, chopped

1 clove garlic, chopped
½ teaspoon ground coriander
Salt and pepper to taste

1. At home, split the eggplant in half and scoop out the inside, leaving about ½ inch of flesh on the hollowed shells. Dice the flesh you have scooped out, then set aside both the shells and the flesh. Lightly sauté the lamb in olive oil with the onion, garlic, and seasonings. Toss with the diced eggplant and sauté 5 minutes longer. Mound the mixture in both halves of the eggplant and wrap the halves individually in foil.

2. Place on the engine with the skin side down. Plan a long trip: the cooking time will be 3 to 5 hours.

Speedy Spedini

This is a classic Italian recipe. Stick these small bread-and-cheese sandwiches onto the mill in your Ferrari, and you'll be looking forward to stopping rather than speeding.

DISTANCE: 40 MILES

One 2-ounce can anchovy fillets
$1/4$ cup chicken stock
1 loaf good-quality Italian bread, about 3 inches in diameter
$3/4$ pound mozzarella, preferably fresh
Butter for greasing foil

1. At home, drain the anchovies and mash with a fork. Add the chicken stock to make a thin paste. Slice the bread into $1/2$-inch rounds, and slice the cheese into $1/4$-inch slices. Make triple-decker sandwiches, using 3 slices of bread and 2 slices of cheese for each, and brushing the inside surfaces of the bread with the anchovy spread. Wrap each sandwich individually in buttered foil.

2. Cook until the cheese is runny, about 45 minutes.

Stuffed Whole Fish

*T*his is quite a production and is probably suited only to a large engine, maybe an inline six with a hefty manifold running along the side. Use any firm-fleshed, nonoily fish. A small striped bass or large red snapper would be ideal. The presentation is much nicer with the head on, but you can take it off if space dictates. Headroom in cars isn't what it used to be.

DISTANCE: 140 MILES

1 stick butter, plus extra for greasing foil
$3/4$ pound fresh mushrooms, minced
1 pound fresh spinach
2 egg whites
Dash of nutmeg
Salt and pepper to taste
1 small red onion, finely minced
1 whole fish, 3 to 4 pounds

1. At home, prepare the stuffing. Melt the butter in a saucepan, and when it foams, add the mushrooms. Stir and reduce the heat to a simmer. Cook, stirring frequently, until the liquid has evaporated and you're left with a creamy mass. Set aside. Rinse the spinach and remove the tough stems, then cook in a small amount of boiling water for 5 to 10 minutes. Drain, pressing out the excess water, then chop very fine. Beat the egg whites until frothy, and then blend with the spinach, adding the nutmeg, salt, pepper, and onion.

2. Place the fish on a cutting board. With a thin boning knife, cut along both sides of the backbone from just behind the head of the fish to the base of the tail until the bone is free. Sever the backbone at both ends of the cut, and lift it out, leaving the two sides of the fish joined at the head and tail.

3. Spread the spinach mixture inside the fish, topping with a layer of the mushroom mixture. Carefully wrap the fish in buttered foil, taking care to preserve its shape.

4. Cook about 2½ hours, turning once (*very carefully*). If you can pull this off, we'll let you contribute to the next edition of *Manifold Destiny*—although, come to think of it, this *is* the next edition, and we're still waiting for someone to check in with a fish story.

THE MIDWEST

The Midwest is where New England's solid Yankee fare took root on enormous prairie farms and in lunch-bucket industrial cities. Long hours spent in the fields or the foundry translated into prodigious appetites, which is how midwestern food got its reputation for density and heft. They don't serve "medallions" of anything here; they serve manhole covers.

What's more, a funny thing happened to midwestern cooking on its way through the nineteenth century. It met up with the least subtle cuisine on earth—that of the Scandinavians and Central Europeans, who came to make machine tools and tend dairy cattle. If you think chicken and dumplings is serious business, how about a couple of pig's knuckles?

For the car-engine cook, the Midwest is hallowed ground. Not only is the native cuisine admirably suited to a cooking method that is imprecise, forgiving, and innocent of fine nuances, but it comes from the very same part of the country that gave us the American car in all its classic glory. And it's great driving country—not for harrowing downshifts on hairpin turns, but for cooking basic fare to the locally esteemed fare-thee-well while barreling down mind-numbing four-hundred-mile straightaways. It's a perfect marriage of taste and terrain.

Just remember: in the Midwest, *dinner* is what you cook in the morning and eat at noon. Later in the day, it's *supper* you're taking off the engine.

Lead-Foot Stuffed Cabbage

Stuffed cabbage is a dish that can be pleasingly filling or as heavy as lead, depending on what goes into it. In this version, the food sociologist can observe the effects of several generations of simplifying Americanization on an old Eastern European favorite. Pop a few of these down your throat while you're pounding down some godforsaken stretch of rust-belt interstate, and the accumulated weight will sink all the way to your right foot.

NOTE: These are best prepared in a ten-year-old Dodge Intrepid with a YOU BETCHA DUPA I'M POLISH sticker on the bumper.

DISTANCE: 55 MILES

1 small green cabbage
1 pound ground beef
1 cup uncooked rice
2 beef bouillon cubes
2 cans condensed tomato soup
Salt and pepper to taste

1. At home, separate the leaves of the cabbage, discarding the tough outer ones and removing the inner ones intact. Drop the leaves into boiling water. After 10 minutes, drain and rinse with cold water.

2. Cook the beef in a skillet, breaking it up with a spoon, until it's no longer pink. Do not drain the fat. Meanwhile, cook the rice in 2 cups of water along with the bouillon cubes until the water is absorbed and the rice is done. Combine the rice, meat, and 1 can of the soup (do not add water), and season with salt and pepper.

3. One by one, lay out a blanched cabbage leaf flat, drop some

stuffing on it, and roll it up, forming a neat bundle with both ends sealed. Repeat until you run out of cabbage or stuffing.

4. Place the rolls on foil in pairs, smearing each with a generous amount of soup from the second can. Wrap.

5. Find a good place for them on the engine and drive about 1 hour, depending on the size of your cabbage leaves.

Candy-Apple-Red Chicken

Why would anyone combine sugar with canned tomato sauce and Worcestershire sauce? Don't ask. A good midwestern guest eats what's put on his plate.

DISTANCE: 85–110 MILES

1 chicken breast, split
1/2 cup chopped onion
1/2 cup chopped green pepper
1/2 teaspoon garlic powder
1 teaspoon oregano
One 6-ounce can tomato sauce
4 teaspoons brown sugar
1 tablespoon Worcestershire sauce
1/4 cup cider vinegar

At home, place each chicken breast half on a sheet of foil. Combine the remaining ingredients and ladle half of the mixture over each breast half. Wrap carefully. Cook 1 1/2 to 2 hours.

Olds Soldiers Never Die
Pepper Steak

The more entrenched a democracy is, the more it seems to develop increasingly ornate social distinctions, most of which are highly visible. Otherwise, what would be the point of having them?

The military, naturally, encourages the class system. Becoming an officer seems to be preordained, and the rewards are visible, whether in housing, transportation, or the possibility of a future, any future. Come retirement time, status clings to those gold-weighted shoulders. Newspapers frequently quote General Thaddeus Windsor Newton (Ret.) about this or that, but when was the last time you encountered words of wisdom from Corporal Ernie Schmursky (Ret.)?

The mouth is connected to the stomach, and armies travel on their stomachs, which brings us to our point, sort of. Officers—especially the retired ones—seem to like big cars, perhaps a throwback to the days of command vehicles. Chevys and Fords are fine for the foot soldiers and the white-capped gobs, but the privileged class certainly likes those cars big enough to warrant a chauffeur. (When General George Patton suffered his fatal injuries, he was a passenger, not the driver, in a Cadillac, and since the war was over, he was hunting pheasants, not peasants.)

What better choice for a lunchtime cruise past the parade grounds than a vintage Oldsmobile Ninety-Eight? A 1972 Ninety-Eight is 232 inches long, which is two inches longer than a Sherman M4 tank, the mainstay of the Allied armies of World War II. Like the old soldiers who fade away, the Olds was at its peak in '72, but it was approaching the end of its era.

The Ninety-Eight went on a yo-yo diet, downsizing in 1977 and 1985, then fattening up again for 1991. It left the world in 1996, followed by the Olds marque itself in 2004, the oldest auto brand in the

United States at the time. That same year Clint Eastwood starred in *Million Dollar Baby;* his character, a has-been boxing trainer, drove an early '80s Ninety-Eight. The movie's ending was no happier than Oldsmobile's.

But what the heck, war is hell, right? This dish is a new version of a previous *Manifold Destiny* entrée based on a favorite of that old favorite himself, the steak au poivre of General Dwight D. Eisenhower (Ret.). To make it easier for the dentally challenged, we've changed the strip steak to a faux burger, easy on the taste buds as well as the choppers, a salute to the fallen and a look forward to the future.

DISTANCE: 55 MILES

1 small baking potato
1 pound ground beef
Salt and pepper to taste
Paprika (See note)
Butter for greasing foil

NOTE: If you're like most of us, you have a jar of paprika at the rear of your spice shelf, purchased back in 1989 for that chicken recipe that didn't quite work out. By now it's utterly taste-free, but still looks pretty. Sprinkle liberally over the patty before sealing. If you eat with your eyes closed you'll never know it's there.

1. Peel the potato and boil until thoroughly cooked through. Cut in half and eat one-half as a snack, with a touch of butter and salt and pepper.

2. Mash the remaining half well, then blend with the ground beef. This is essential for proper military texture. Trust us.

3. Form the beef mixture into 8 patties and sprinkle with salt, pepper, and paprika. Triple-wrap in buttered foil and stuff onto available engine hot spots.

4. Stop once to turn the patties. Keep the beef juices away from your dress uniform.

Hot Dog Surprise

*T*he surprise is that people still cook these. We first encountered them back in Cub Scout days, back when they were making not only Oldsmobiles but DeSotos, Ramblers . . . no, not Packards. We're not that old.

DISTANCE: 40 MILES

10 hot dogs
American cheese (or boutique-brand Vermont Cheddar, if you have
     an expensive car), sliced into hot dog–length fingers
10 slices bacon

1. At home or on the road, cut a deep slit in each wiener, and stuff with fingers of cheese. Then wrap on the diagonal, like an old bias-ply tire, with the bacon. Seal individually in foil.

2. These are great for stuffing into those odd places on the engine where you can't fit a turkey or a suckling pig. Cook about 45 minutes or until the cheese is melted and the bacon is somewhat crisp.

Out-of-the-Fire, Onto-the-Engine Stew

When we were lads, we both belonged to chapters of a uniformed organization devoted to woodcraft, knot tying, and discipline. Looking back, we realize that the major purpose of this tent-raising and marching society was to keep boys occupied until they were old enough to drive. It's probably significant that the only conceivable activity they didn't award a badge for was driving.

Leafing through some of the recipes that got us through long, tedious, bug-bitten outings back in our paramilitary prepubescence, we came up with this number, ideally suited to motorized hiking. Put it on your engine and see if anyone salutes.

DISTANCE: 85 MILES

4 ounces meat (any kind), cut into ¹/₂-inch dice
3 vegetables you like (potatoes, carrots, onions, celeriac, etc.),
    cut into ¹/₂-inch dice
Salt and pepper to taste

1. At home or on the road, mix all the ingredients and wrap.
2. Originally, we cooked this on the coals of a campfire, but since we're all grown-ups now, put it on the engine and drive for 1¹/₂ hours, turning at least once. (Don't blame us; it wasn't our idea to begin with.)

Cruise-Control Pork Tenderloin

*T*his is about as fancy as you dare get in the down-home Midwest, but it's okay if the pork tenderloin is from a native Iowa hog. The long cooking time will let you put a lot of prairie miles behind you. Just set the cruise control, line up your hood ornament with a distant landmark, like the Nebraska State Capitol, and set a timer to wake you up when dinner is ready.

DISTANCE: 250 MILES

3 tablespoons Dijon mustard
2 tablespoons dry white wine
1/2 red onion, minced
2 teaspoons rosemary, crushed
Salt and pepper to taste
1 pork tenderloin, 1 to 1 1/2 pounds, butterflied
Olive oil for greasing foil

1. At home or on the road, blend the mustard, wine, onion, and seasonings. Spread the split surface of the tenderloin with the mixture and press lightly together, then wrap in foil that has been lightly oiled (olive oil is best).

2. Find a medium-hot spot on the engine and turn once during cooking. Total cooking time should be about 4 1/2 hours.

Any-City Chicken Wings

By now, "Buffalo" chicken wings have been consumed by millions who have no idea where Buffalo is, or that it is the threshold of the great Midwest. This is perfectly fine, since none of the bar cooks who make them—or who thaw them out and heat them—know where it is either. This recipe is based on the premise that since you can call something anything you want, you can also put anything you want into it.

DISTANCE: 140–200 MILES

18 chicken wings
½ cup ketchup
1 cup red wine vinegar
4 to 6 canned jalapeño peppers, drained and minced (more if you like
   wings really hot)
3 cloves garlic, minced
1 tablespoon oregano
1 teaspoon red pepper flakes
Salt to taste

1. At home, place the chicken wings in a bowl. Blend the remaining ingredients in a second bowl, pour over the wings, and stir to thoroughly coat the wings. Cover tightly and refrigerate for 24 hours, stirring occasionally. Drain the wings, retaining the marinating liquid, and divide them among 3 sheets of foil. Brush with the reserved marinade.

2. Cook from Buffalo to Ashtabula, Ohio, if you know where either city is. Total cooking time will be about 2½ hours. If they aren't done at Ashtabula, press on to Cleveland (another hour down I-90).

Made with a 'Slade in the Shade

We saw our first luxe version of a sports ute in Times Square in the summer of 1997. It was a Lincoln Navigator, slurping its way across Seventh Avenue on a lovely summer day. We're over six feet in heels, yet found ourselves at eye level with a suited gentleman aiming fifty-six hundred pounds of assorted metal. He, in turn, seeing an instant smirk spread across one more New Yorker's face, hit the button and up went the tinted window. Such is life in the jungle.

It was our introduction to the pimped version of an SUV, one of the most crazed American automotive trends since lethal tail fins, the canonization of a vehicle that no more serves its avowed purpose than mice enjoy cats as neighbors. Later we realized that the *U* stands for upholstered rather than utility, and life became easier to understand.

Our current star of the genre is the Caddy Escalade, which makes the Navigator look demure, almost prissy. Everything we can see of the 'Slade is too big, too pudgy—the village fat man in hand-sewn tight yellow pants. Yet a certain slice of the American pie goes gooey over the thing. Last October Bob Dylan spent a day on his satellite radio show playing only songs with Cadillac references. He also drives one in a television commercial. (It could be worse—Mr. Dylan endorsed Victoria's Secret too, but he didn't model the goods.)

We checked out the possibilities for the Caddy, and found out why we see so many of them at the country club rather than checking in at the local check-in station during the deer season. The one option not listed in the sales material is dirt.

But since we're counting, we'll start with "Blue Chip" for the exterior finish. We considered "Gold Mist" but decided it was too, well, attention-getting. Just kidding, folks. We'll take the "six-speed transmission with driver shift control" so we can pretend we're in charge, and "road-sensing suspension" seems useful for those times when we lose ours. Everyone likes a warm place to sit while cruising, so we'll get the "heated and cooled seats" (don't forget the summer), the "heated steering wheel," "heated washer fluid," since our windshield doesn't like a cold shower any more than we do, and, finally, the "engine-block heater," oddly the only option that costs extra, although only seventy-five bucks. Tough guys have nothing to prove, especially in the depths of winter.

A proper lunch cooked on an Escalade should fulfill one automotive critic's description of the pull-toy itself, "a Chevy truck in a mink stole." It calls out for a filling of rich European tradition, with the whole thing slathered onto a chassis of utterly drab stodginess.

A few pages back, we recalled a favorite dish from Cub Scout days—fingers of American cheese inserted into longitudinally sliced hot dogs, which were then wrapped in foil and stuck in the campfire. Our scoutmaster was our fearless leader, showing us the man's way of dealing with the elements.

Now the fearless leader has morphed into a heavyset bond trader who exercises only on weekends. But he's still the leader of his pack, and now we have more cash for supplies.

DISTANCE: 50 MILES

1 handful of Manchego cheese (imported, naturally; pick the most
   expensive), cut into long fingers, 1/4 inch thick and wide
1 bag of thick-cut frozen French fries, opened and thawed
4 ounces top-of-the-line prosciutto, sliced thin (If available, use Serrano
   ham, which is even more costly.)

1. To assemble, make small bundles of sticks of cheese and potato (sort of like making your own fasces). Wrap well in slices of ham.

2. Wrap tightly in foil, and place on the hottest part of the engine you can find. Drive about an hour, or until you can smell the ham and cheese.

3. Serve with plenty of napkins (linen, please, this is a **Cadillac,** with leather seats), and remember, the alpha male dines first! Plus, it's his ride.

Milwaukee Memory Mittagessen*

One of us used to live in Milwaukee, back when the Teutonic flavor of the place was still richly pervasive. The big downtown hotels were the Pfister and the Schroeder; city officials had names like Zeidler, Maier, and Brier; the Blatz brewery was still in business; the classiest restaurants weren't trendy fusion or "New American" joints but Ratzschs's, Mader's (both survive), and the late lamented John Ernst Cafe; the flowers on the downtown median strips grew in precise rows; and if you jaywalked, people looked at you as if you had violated the social contract. Best of all, the Milwaukee branch of the old Gimbel's department store chain devoted almost its entire first floor to aisle after aisle of Mitteleuropa comestibles that you purchased from iron-coiffed ladies in white lab coats. If you didn't want to walk all the way to the Usinger's sausage factory (also, *danke Gott*, still in business), you could stock up at Gimbel's on the best wurst in town, along with pickled herring, boat-anchor loaves of rye bread, German potato salad, heaps of sauerkraut, and tortes that were indistinguishable from felonies.

It's in the old Milwaukee spirit that we offer this automotive take on a classic German dinner. Ideally, you should cook it on the '63 Opel Kadett that you've kept in mint condition, on a drive along the lake on the North Side, where the beer barons' mansions are.

DISTANCE: 60–75 MILES

4 ounces sauerkraut (If you can't find a German specialty shop that sells it in bulk, buy the canned product imported from Germany.)

1 small potato, grated

1/2 teaspoon caraway seeds

* "Lunch," *auf Deutsch.*

3 tablespoons dry white wine
2 *weisswurst* (fine-grained veal sausage), slit in half

At home, stir together the sauerkraut, grated potato, caraway seeds, and wine. Arrange a nest of the kraut mixture on foil and arrange the slit sausages on top, covering with more kraut. Wrap carefully, so juices don't leak. Cook on a medium-hot spot on the engine, and wash down with . . . well, not with Blatz anymore, but they still make Leinenkugel up in Chippewa Falls.

Winnebago Welfare Wiggle

Somewhere back in the '50s, Mom came across a recipe for shrimp and green peas napped in a hollandaise sauce. It was called "Shrimp Wiggle," a title that, our research suggests, was derived from the putative wiggliness of the main ingredient when they were still alive. (The name went over well in the Midwest, we assume, since folks there no doubt looked at headless, legless, canned, or frozen supermarket shrimp and figured them for the kind of creatures that might wiggle, like bait.)

But shrimp were way too uptown for Mom, and hollandaise belonged in Holland, somewhere over there, across the ocean. Thus tuna wiggle: having lived through the Depression meant that another one was always possible, at a moment's notice, such as before your next meal. Hence, you'd better make sure your last meal was a cheap one, just in case.

In 1950, Chrysler's now-defunct Plymouth division ran an ad touting the fact that if you factored in all the options and colors they had available, there were three thousand ways to build a Plymouth. That was pretty good for one of the era's "low-priced three" (with Chevy and Ford), but far too fancy for the wiggle crowd that made up the three's prime demographic. When you added up the options and colors available in tuna wiggle, you still came out with only one way to make it. Unless, of course, you used canned shrimp, you class traitor.

We did not, by the way, name this recipe after the town in Wisconsin. It's named after the vehicle—a great, wiggle-friendly housing option for the next Depression.

DISTANCE: 55–1,000 MILES

1 package frozen green peas
1 can chunk light tuna in oil, drained and flaked

1. At home or on the road, thaw the peas enough so they can be separated. In a mixing bowl—or in a clean hubcap—combine the peas and the tuna. Dump the glop on a sheet of foil and make a reasonably neat package.

2. Throw it on the engine and cook about 1 hour. The peas *should* be overdone.

NOTE: Since this makes a relatively soft package, it's ideal for molding around various odd shapes.

To Grandmother's House Road Turkey

*U*nless you haul the family around at holiday time in a Greyhound bus, you'd be pretty hard-pressed to engine-roast a whole turkey on the way to the in-laws'. These individual portions will not only solve the space problem; when they're done, they'll keep the kids amused in the backseat. Afterward, cleaning up the mess can be turned into a family game, with extra cookies for the one who finds the most shards of foil in the upholstery. (Keep the used foil away from the dog if you want to have a happy holiday.)

DISTANCE: 220 MILES

1 boneless turkey breast, about 5 pounds, sliced into thin strips against the grain
3 large baking potatoes, peeled and diced
3 carrots, finely diced
Dry white wine
Flour for dredging
Butter for greasing foil
Salt and pepper to taste
3/4 cup heavy cream

1. At home, combine the turkey, potatoes, and carrots in a bowl with wine to cover. Marinate for 2 hours in the refrigerator, then drain well (*don't* drink the wine). Setting the vegetables aside, dredge the turkey pieces in flour, then heavily butter 5 large squares of foil. Arrange equal amounts of turkey and vegetables on each square, and season with salt and pepper as desired. Cup the foil around the turkey and vegetables, and pour over each serving as much heavy cream as you can without making a soupy mess, then seal carefully.

2. Cook on the engine about 4 hours, turning once. We're assuming that Grandma doesn't live in the next town.

THE SOUTH

For every culinary action, there's an equal reaction. There's no mystery as to why southern cooking has become wildly popular among the hip foodie set—it's simply that you can spend only so much time on your high horse, preaching and practicing refined, nutritionally sound eating habits, without hankering for what is euphemistically called "comfort food." The stalwarts of the eat-right crowd might like to trumpet the virtues of, say, the Mediterranean diet (a crock, since real Mediterranean types live on mortadella and cheese, bake bread with pork cracklings in it, and fry squash blossoms in batter), but they love to go off the wagon and scarf down barbecue, hush puppies, country ham, and all the other caloric delights they watch plump Confederates rustle up on the Food Network. They're like those politicians and televangelists who rail against sins of the flesh, and then get caught in cheap motels, or plush Washington hotels, with comely entrepreneurs—only the southern/comfort food yearning doesn't even have to be kept secret.

Toss in the ethnic influences of Hispanic Miami and French New Orleans, and you've got calories that have turned trendy and respectable. And, because this is a cuisine that is nothing if not simple, much of it is admirably suited to cooking à la car.

Median Noche

The sandwich called the *medianoche* is a South Florida staple. It was brought to our shores by Cuban exiles, who presumably had fond memories of eating *medianoches* at midnight (that's what the Spanish word means) during a night on the town in old Havana, back before the revolution made nights on the town a scarce commodity for anyone not directly benefiting from a trickle-down of rubles. Hemingway probably liked to wolf down a *medianoche* somewhere between his tenth and eleventh *mojito*.

The *medianoche* is actually a subspecies of the ubiquitous sandwich Cubano, which is stuffed with ham, roast pork, cheese, and pickles, then pressed (sort of like panini, but without the grill marks) and served hot. The *medianoche* version differs in that it's usually made with a sweeter, softer, flakier variety of the traditional thin-crusted Cuban bread. Pressing, of course, is the key to making one of these filling little numbers on a car engine—what you want is a flat, cast-aluminum injector housing, tight hood clearance (the foil-cone test and foil wadding is a must here), and a hot night to get it done right. It would be great if you could make these on one of those lovingly preserved '50s hulks that lumber around Havana, but they have carburetors and air filters atop their engines, and you'd never get the pressing right. Plus, you'd have to go to Havana, which would piss off the State Department.

Our variant gets its name, of course, from our recommended dining venue. Around midnight, just pull onto the median and eat.

DISTANCE: 40–50 MILES

Mustard
8-inch length Cuban bread with hard crust (or French bread),
        cut lengthwise in half
4 thin slices ham

4 thin slices roast pork (This is a good way to use leftovers from that
    pork loin you roasted for dinner.)
4 thin slices Swiss cheese
4 slices pickle (slice lengthwise)
Butter for greasing foil

1. Spread mustard on both halves of the bread. For filling layers, start with the ham, then the pork, then the cheese, and finish with the pickle slices. Cover with the top half of the bread and wrap tightly in buttered foil. (Some aficionados butter the bread on the outside; for our variation, you can just butter the foil.)

2. Find that special spot on the engine, and make sure you get good pressing action. Turn once during cooking. For some reason, *medianoche* sandwiches are traditionally cut corner to corner, so you get two elongated right-triangle-shaped portions.

Good and Simple Cajun Shrimp/Crayfish

Driving down a highway like old U.S. 90, which goes east-west through Louisiana, you'll see lots of trucks in parking lots selling shrimp, crabs, and, if the season's right, crayfish. Stop and buy some, then go to the nearest vegetable stand and get some garlic, onions, and small green hot peppers. Now get cooking.

DISTANCE: 35 MILES

6 small green hot peppers
1 medium onion
2 cloves garlic
1 pound shrimp or crayfish, in their shells (if using shrimp, remove legs)
Butter for greasing foil

1. At home or on the road, remove the seeds from the peppers (a good reason to keep rubber gloves in your car) and mince finely, along with the onion and garlic. Spread the shrimp or crayfish on heavily buttered foil and cover with the vegetables. Wrap.

2. Cook about 40 minutes, until the shellfish are nice and pink. Cooking them in their shells adds flavor and gives you something to lick afterward.

"Cajun" Shrimp

Once, while driving through Louisiana, we stopped to check out the shelves in a Pick and Pay supermarket in Lake Arthur. It was the first time we ever saw *gallon* jars of rendered pork fat in a butcher's case. Next we browsed through the condiment and spice selections, and realized that a lot of what was then sweeping the country as "Cajun" cooking increasingly comes out of jars—jars of precooked roux, jars of spice mixes for meat and fish, jars with drawings of fat men on them. In short, what started out as a bona fide regional cuisine had become a regional abomination designed to make fat people fatter. We don't know what the life expectancy is down there, but we do know that it's possible to travel through Cajun country for a week without encountering any food that isn't fried, with the exception of coffee and salad. Here's a sample, with the brand names deleted.

DISTANCE: 55 MILES

Rendered pork fat
1 pound shrimp from the supermarket
Assorted jars of whatever "Cajun" seasonings you've seen advertised

1. At home or on the road, heat the fat until it liquefies. If you're a real die-hard car cook, you might want to do this on an idling engine, using one of the cleaned-out tuna cans you keep on hand to make Eggs-On Cheese Pie (page 61). Peel the shrimp and devein them if they're large. Then dredge the shrimp in the fat and dust heavily with the powdered spices. Wrap.

2. Place on a medium-hot part of the engine, and cook about 1 hour. It doesn't matter if the shrimp are overcooked, since you're eating a concept, not a food.

Orange Roughly Floribbean

Charles Darwin had to sign on to the *Beagle* for a no-frills world cruise in order to come up with the theory of natural selection. But we've got it easy: for incontrovertible proof that evolution is still humming along, all we have to do is go to the fish department in the supermarket. How else to explain entire new species of fish? For instance, who the hell ever heard of tilapia until a few years ago? We would have thought it was some crummy little town in a Faulkner novel—but no, it's apparently a new piscatorial development.

Same with orange roughy, the star of this recipe. When we first heard it mentioned, we were sure the reference was to a Protestant hoodlum in Belfast. It is, of course, a mild, firm-fleshed fish that fillets nicely—but when we looked through *My First Book of Fishes*, the standard work we've consulted for years, there was nary an orange roughy to be found.

Anyway, orange roughy turns out to be perfectly suited for the "Floribbean" treatment, that Miami-based trend that involves tossing together fresh local fish, tropical produce, and, in many cases, sugar's lunge at greatness, a.k.a. the Demon Rum. This is a dish to cook on the engine of a snazzy convertible while driving along Collins Avenue in Miami Beach, past art deco hotels that have the same color scheme as your dinner.

DISTANCE: 40 MILES

    Juice of 1 lime
    1/2 jalapeño or 1/4 Scotch bonnet pepper, minced (use rubber gloves)
    2 orange roughy fillets, about 1/2 pound total
    Butter for greasing foil
    1 yellow banana pepper, cut into thin strips
    2 tablespoons dark rum

1. At home, squeeze the lime juice into a shallow bowl big enough to marinate the fish. Add the minced hot pepper, then place the fish in the lime-pepper marinade and turn. Marinate the fish for 30 minutes, turning once.

2. Lightly butter foil, and lay down half of the banana pepper strips. Splash 1 tablespoon of the rum on the pepper. Remove the fish from the marinade, taking along as much of the hot pepper bits as you care to, and place it atop the pepper. Arrange the remainder of the banana pepper over the fish, and splash with the rest of the rum. Wrap. Wedge into a hot spot and turn once during cooking.

NOTE: Divide the ingredients and prepare in two packets if the engine requires.

U.S. 17 Carolina Stuffed Crabs

This solves the problem of live ones scurrying off the engine.

DISTANCE: 40–55 MILES

6 large blue crabs
5 tablespoons butter
15 sprigs fresh parsley, chopped
3 scallions, chopped
2 cups stale bread crumbs
Juice of 1 lemon

1. At home, boil the crabs. Pick through the meat and remove the cartilage, reserving the shells. Melt 2 tablespoons of the butter in a saucepan and sauté the parsley and scallions until limp. Add the crabmeat and heat briefly. Add the bread crumbs, lemon juice, and enough cold water to make a moist, firm stuffing. Fill the crab shells, dot with the remaining butter, and wrap.

2. Bake in medium-hot engine crannies 45 minutes to 1 hour.

Pickup Ham Steak

A lot of southern cooking, especially in the "comfort" category, seems to include staples like margarine and cheese. We're not saying it's good; we're saying it's there.

DISTANCE: 85 MILES

1 ham steak
Margarine for greasing foil
1 cup canned tomatoes, drained
4 ounces unsliced American cheese, grated
1 small onion, minced
1 bay leaf
2 tablespoons minced parsley
Pepper to taste
$\frac{1}{4}$ teaspoon thyme

1. At home, place the ham steak on margarined foil. Combine all of the other ingredients, spread over the ham, and seal tightly.

2. This can be a messy one. When you size up the cooking spots your engine affords, go for security rather than maximum heat—it's a perfect recipe for foil-wedging on top of a cast-aluminum injector housing, or nestling in along the side of a valve cover on an old V8. Cook about 1½ hours; if it needs more time, leave the engine running while you stop in at a roadhouse for a Jim Beam and Co'Cola.

Maryland Crab-Imperial

We once had an assignment from a prestigious newspaper—the one that brought down the Nixon administration—to do a story that involved visiting every accessible lighthouse on Chesapeake Bay (even prestigious newspapers have to go slumming sometimes). The assignment turned into a one-thousand-mile *tour de crabe*, as we hit one joint after another that specialized in the bay's most famous denizens. Not counting soft-shells, which are a seasonal item relating to the creatures' molting schedules, we found that the vast majority of Chesapeake crabs tend to find their way onto the plate in one of three ways: boiled and served on a big sheet of brown paper with a mallet and pick; fried with batter as crab cakes or fritters; and—generally in places that have cloth napkins—in the casserole known as crab imperial.

As long as the basic recipe is sound, this is a nice way to eat crabs. The brown-paper mallet-and-pick approach is not only messy, but guilt-inducing: when you survey the pile of debris left after a hearty feed, you feel as if you've single-handedly put the crustaceans on the endangered species list. As for crab cakes and fritters, you're at the mercy of cooks who hold up a crab so it can pee on a big blob of batter, which is then fried without further crab participation. But you can't really fake crab imperial, and you don't have to think about how many crabs actually went into a decent portion.

We have no idea where this dish got its imperialist name. But maybe you should cook it on an old Chrysler Imperial.

DISTANCE: 50 MILES

1 pound blue crabmeat, picked over
$^1/_2$ green bell pepper, diced
1 pimiento, diced
Pinch of salt

A few gratings of white pepper
1 teaspoon dry mustard (mild, not Chinese hot)
2 tablespoons heavy cream
1 tablespoon dry sherry
1 egg, lightly beaten
Butter for greasing foil

1. At home or on the road, mix all the ingredients together, being careful not to break the crabmeat into tiny shreds.

2. Butter a sheet of foil. Mound the crab mixture on the foil and wrap carefully—make sure the final two wraps are tight enough to hold this fairly loose mixture, but make the package malleable enough so that it can be molded onto an appropriate engine surface (preferably one of the hotter ones). The dish is done when the egg has set.

New Orleans Carpetbagger Steak

We wanted to call our New Orleans recipe "Hell of a Job Brownies," but there's no getting around the fact that you can't bake on a car engine. Our next idea was to honor some of the humbler culinary traditions of the beleaguered Big Easy, with a nod to the great Buster Holmes. Until about 1981, Buster—who died in 1994—ran a wonderfully unpretentious little joint, named after himself, on the corner of Burgundy and Orleans streets in an out-of-the-way corner of the Vieux Carré. Buster's place was a timeworn temple of red beans and rice, served up with sausage, turkey wings, or maybe rabbit or duck. The trouble with a Buster Holmes homage, though—at least for our purposes—was that traditional New Orleans recipes like his require long cooking, as well as real pots on real stoves.

So we decided to resurrect a nineteenth-century dish with a name appropriate to the social climate of post-Katrina New Orleans. Keep in mind that we're going against our own caveat about car-engine grilling here: you can seldom expect to get a nice, browned surface on a steak using our methods, but there's always the chance that you have a car with just the right hot horizontal surface, and can defy the laws of probability. After all, we *did* brown those game hens on the '88 Chrysler (page 21) on that long-ago drive up the Maine coast.

Warning: If you find an '88 Chrysler on the market, just make sure it didn't come from New Orleans.

DISTANCE: 30–50 MILES, DEPENDING ON ENGINE HEAT
AND DEGREE OF DONENESS DESIRED

1 cup fresh oysters, drained and chopped
1/2 cup chopped fresh mushrooms
2 teaspoons chopped fresh parsley
3 tablespoons melted butter

4 slices bacon, cooked and crumbled
1 ounce crumbled blue cheese
¹/₄ cup dry white wine
4 rib eye steaks, about 1 inch thick

1. At home, sauté the oysters, mushrooms, and parsley in the butter until the mushrooms are tender; drain. Stir in the bacon, cheese, and wine; set aside.

2. Make pockets in the sides of the steaks and stuff with the oyster mixture. Wrap tightly so that the stuffing is firmly secured within the steaks. Place the packages (one steak to a package; halve the recipe if there isn't enough room) flat against the hottest part of the engine, and turn halfway through your drive.

CALIFORNIA AND THE WEST

All cuisine west of the prairies and south of the Red River—that's the Texas-Oklahoma boundary—used to be summed up in a few simple clichés: steaks on the grill, chili and other Tex-Mex standbys, seafood in the Northwest. Southern California, back before the invention of its signature cuisine, was just another grilled T-bone sort of place. Take a look at a photo of stars at a garden party circa 1950: those aren't Vietnamese spring rolls they're eating.

Things started to get more complicated when the first slice of avocado was slipped onto a hamburger, and "California cuisine" was born. Later permutations (which often involved dropping the hamburger) made more and more of a fetish of the hyperfresh, the preciously obscure, and the quirkily juxtaposed—Wolfgang Puck, remember, first made his name by constructing pizzas out of ingredients no Neapolitan ever dreamed of—back in the '70s when the rest of us were still grilling avocadoless burgers whose association with the word *puck* had more to do with Canada's national sport.

Even simple southwestern fare got a sophisticated overhaul, requiring cooks to get master's degrees in peppers. Back in 1982, we found a recipe for forty pounds of chili that inspired us to throw a big party. We had to improvise, though, when we couldn't find anyone—not even after frantic calls to Texans—who knew what "chipotles" were. Now it's the name of a restaurant chain.

But we've come full circle, and the grill is once again the star of the show—or the show-off of the stars, from the look of some of the propane-fired extravaganzas that serve as the centerpieces of full-fledged outdoor kitchens. Even mere mortals can go to Costco and buy gas grills bigger than their cars, which of course raises the question: why not just cook on your car in the first place?

Ford F-150 Hot Texas Wieners

Ford's F-Series pickup trucks celebrated their sixtieth anniversary in 2008. We were looking through a commemorative volume on the series recently and noticed a funny thing about the progression of pickup-truck advertising over the years. The early F-1s were invariably depicted in work situations—orchard workers loading bushels of peaches, warehousemen hefting machine parts into a pickup bed, even two guys delivering beehives. This motif continued up until the late '60s, when the ads shifted in a direction they've taken ever since. Now the trucks were shown more and more in situations where people were having fun. They were lifestyle vehicles now, and Ford must have figured that buyers, after schlepping peaches and machinery and beehives all week, wanted to fantasize about what they and their trucks would be doing on Saturday.

This puts pickups squarely in the realm of engine cooking, since we're all more likely to experiment with using that big Triton V8 to make lunch on a fishing trip or a drive to the NASCAR track rather than during that measly hour the boss gives you before it's back to the beehives. But what to cook? Ford answered that question for us by revealing, somewhere in the publicity surrounding their "King Ranch" edition F-150, that the Southwest is their prime selling area. So, we decided that the pickup meal par excellence should be Hot Texas Wieners. Never mind that they aren't called that in Texas (it's a northern New Jersey term for a hot dog delicacy elsewhere known as a "Michigan," for some unfathomable reason). The Texas connection comes from the use of a beefy chili sauce as the wiener's topping.

Traditionally, the dog is deep-fried, and the sauce is slathered on top over mustard and chopped onions. In our version, the dog is cooked in the sauce. Who said we were hidebound traditionalists?

DISTANCE: 30–50 MILES

The sauce (prepare at home):
- $1/2$ medium onion, finely chopped
- 1 clove garlic, finely chopped
- 2 tablespoons olive oil
- $1/2$ pound ground beef
- 1 teaspoon chili powder
- 1 teaspoon paprika
- $1/2$ teaspoon ground cumin
- $1/4$ to $1/2$ teaspoon cayenne, depending on how peppy you want the sauce
- Salt and pepper to taste
- One 8-ounce can tomato paste, diluted with $1/2$ cup water
- 4 to 6 hot dogs
- 4 to 6 hot dog buns

1. Sauté the onion and garlic in the olive oil until translucent; do not brown. Add the beef and stir until finely crumbled and cooked throughout. Drain off most of the grease; keep some for flavor. Add the seasonings, stir, then add the tomato paste. Simmer over low heat until the flavors are blended, about 45 minutes; add a small amount of water if necessary to prevent sticking or burning. The sauce should be thick, not runny.

2. Place a small amount of sauce on a piece of foil. Place a hot dog atop the sauce and cover with more sauce. Wrap carefully (all three layers of foil are especially important here). Repeat with the remaining hot dogs (the amount of sauce you want on each dog will determine the number of packages you make) and place on the engine in places where the packages will not tear. When done, unwrap so that you can invert the contents of each package into a bun.

3. An alternative method is to prepare the dogs, buns, and all before wrapping, but this may result in soggier buns unless you position the packages so that the buns face up.

4. Wipe your hands on your jeans. Avoid staining King Ranch leather upholstery.

Prius Pork

Unless they were trying to tell us that only a car like this could help prius off our oil dependency, here's another example of goofy, totally arbitrary Japanese car naming. Just think—if the committee had grabbed two more Scrabble tiles out of the bag, we could have been tooling past the pump in something called a Priapus. (We would have stood up to the challenge, of course, and come up with a nice Greek sausage recipe.)

But seriously now. Attention must be paid to this car, which not only uses less gas but makes a statement about one's commitment to Being a Better Person. Even Larry David's alter ego (we hope it's not his real ego) on *Curb Your Enthusiasm* drives a Prius, and he's otherwise committed to Being a Terrible Person.

Priuses have indeed become ubiquitous in Hollywood, where eco-chic is so hot that Arnold Schwarzenegger actually converted one of his Hummers to run on hydrogen. The only thing more eco-chic is to drive a pure electric vehicle, like George Clooney will be doing when he takes delivery of his new Tesla (a name taken not from the Scrabble tile bag but from the Serbian physicist). But George is hardly the first entertainment figure to drive an electric car. In Disney comic books from the '50s, Grandma Duck zipped around Duckburg in a circa 1910 Baker Electric.

What better main ingredient for a Prius recipe than pork? The pig is the hybrid farm animal par excellence—not in the genetic sense, but because it runs on whatever you care to feed it. Pigs will eat anything, from rattlesnakes to garbage from vegan restaurants. That quality alone would have made them a great source for hybrid car names, though we doubt if the Toyota Swinus would have been a big seller.

Just remember, the gas engine on a Prius is the unit on the left when you open the hood.

¹/₄ cup hoisin sauce

2 tablespoons Chinese garlic sauce

¹/₂ pound pork tenderloin, cut diagonally into ³/₄-inch slices

10 to 12 dried black Chinese mushrooms (often sold under the
    appealing name "black fungus") soaked in warm water
    until soft and thinly sliced

Beef or chicken broth as needed

1. At home, combine the two sauces and toss the pork and mushrooms in the mixture; thin with broth if necessary, but don't thin it too much or the packages may leak. Wrap carefully.

2. Turn once during cooking, unless the packages are surrounded on two sides by medium-hot engine surfaces.

Poached Fish Pontiac

*P*ontiac, once it was delivered from its one-flight-up-from-Chevy status by the marketing genius of the late John Z. DeLorean, was a car that had a youthful, wide-open-west, Southern California image. Along with their Trans Ams and GTOs, they even had models with names like Catalina and Bonneville. But today, along with the venerable Grand Prix (which sounds European but is the farthest thing from), the old marque's offerings have names like Torrent, Solstice, and Vibe. The closest Pontiac has come in recent years to a place-specific name is "Aztek," a car so ugly it deserves to be held down on a stone altar and have its still-beating engine cut out with an obsidian knife. Worst of all, the latest entries from this GM division are called "G5," "G6," and "G8," which sound like government pay scales. Old John Z. must be spinning in his grave, somewhere around redline at 6,000 rpm.

Make this recipe on a G8 if you must. But for best results, get hold of a '64 Catalina and head west through Topanga Canyon, hanging a right on Route 1 at Malibu for a drive up the coast.

DISTANCE: 40 MILES

Butter for greasing foil
1 thick fillet of firm white fish native to Pacific waters or 1 halibut steak, about 3/4 pound
3 to 4 tablespoons dry vermouth or white wine
1 teaspoon minced shallots
1 bay leaf (California preferred)
White pepper to taste

1. At home or on the road, lay out a sheet of foil and butter it lightly. Place the fish on the foil, then tuck up the sides of the foil and sprinkle the vermouth or wine over the fish. Spread the shallots on top, then add the bay leaf, pepper, and a few dabs of butter. Close the foil carefully and wrap tightly.

2. Cooking time is approximately 45 minutes, assuming you've found a medium-hot spot (check after 30 minutes if the package is in direct contact with the exhaust manifold). The halibut steak will take longer than the fillet.

Quail à la Veep

We have nothing against hunting, with its bracing fresh air, the thrill of outwitting a wily prey on its home court, and the hunger-inducing smells of the evening's meal. The only part that mystifies us is the hunt as a useless social event, a *danse macabre* employing as many servants as possible to make the job of killing as many small birds as possible as effortless as possible.

We're presenting this scenario strictly as a dramatic possibility, born at the confluence of much money with more power, set down in a land capable of supporting little aside from some reptiles and small birds.

Call it South Texas, for want of a better name, and imagine a weekend afternoon, the sunlight fading as the "shooters," accompanied by outriders working as beaters, try to get in their last shots at scurrying quail, little game birds about the size of pigeons. It's been a long day, broken by a lunch where some may have had a beer, or, maybe, didn't. Do we care? Of course not. Like so many storytellers, we're just making this up as we go.

Perhaps there was a quick trip back to the main house "to freshen up" before manning the guns again. All this riding around—drivers provided, of course—really wears one down after a while. But no matter—quick, there's a rising covey, backlit by the lowering sun! Kablam! One down! Whoops, it's one of ours!

Darn! Call the doctors, call the ambulance, off to the hospital. A hostess of the afternoon might say it's just "a bunch of little bitty pellets," and who's to argue? We certainly weren't there, which may be why we're alive to joke about these things.

We might describe the victim as "yakking and cracking jokes," but of course that might have been after he had been flown to a larger hospital, and before he might have had further side effects, a heart attack, for instance, but only a minor one of course.

And don't forget, in our screenplay he was only hit, going vertically, in his rib cage, shoulder, neck, and face. And these were only flesh wounds, mind you, bird shot from a 28-gauge shotgun. Keep in mind that in Texas certain hunting accidents don't have to be reported. Perhaps it has something to do with who's having the accident. We're just guessing, of course.

The oddest thing about our dream hunt is that after all this work, they served us roast beef for dinner. We have absolutely no memory of anyone hitting a cow.

Maybe they just didn't have a recipe for quail. Try ours.

DISTANCE: WE'RE CHECKING WITH THE SECRET SERVICE

Per serving:

  2 quail, gutted
  1 strip bacon
  Salt and pepper to taste
  2 slices firm, good-quality bread
  Butter for greasing foil

1. Rinse the quail and wipe dry. Cut the bacon strip in half and stuff each bird cavity with one piece. Sprinkle with salt and pepper, and place each bird right side up, that is, breast side down, on a slice of bread. Wrap well in buttered foil and place in the hottest spot you can find on the engine.

2. Serve with the bread slices as cooking juice sponges.

Donner Pass Red Flannel Hash

Say you're hanging out at your country place in the hills of Nixon, Nevada, and feel like having a soda. It's the weekend and a couple of friends from the East are visiting, so why not give them a taste of the countryside and head to Soda Springs, over the line in California? Take 447 down to I-80 and head west into the Sierra Nevada. Maybe you should take your new Chevy Tahoe, since Soda Springs is only about twenty-five miles northwest of that mile-and-more-high lake. But before you go, you might want to think about lunch.

For between you and Soda Springs is the 7,000-foot Donner Pass. With the sturdy Tahoe, you'll be tempted to take the back road, old Route 40, also known as the Donner Pass Road—what are four-wheel drives for, after all? While I-80 gets closed only for about five days each winter, Route 40 shuts down "every day there's a snow-storm," according to the California Highway Patrol unit at Truckee.

Keep the gas tank topped off, and bring some blankets—you never know how long you'll have to keep warm, waiting for the search party. And have provisions on hand, or you might be forced to make a substantial philosophical decision. We all know what happened at Donner Pass. How well do you want to know your friends?

The nice thing about hash is that you can make it with just about any kind of meat that's available. Also, we figure that in winter, a red flannel shirt is a standard part of the layered look, so we included beets. If you haven't brought them along, just toss in a piece of the shirt for color.

DRIVING (OR IDLING) TIME: UNTIL YOU'RE REALLY HUNGRY

1 pound meat (beef, turkey, chicken, corned beef, or whatever is
    available), cubed
1 pound potatoes (or whatever wild root vegetable might be within
    arm's reach of the car), cubed

1 large onion (or maybe some wild ramps from under the snow),
  chopped
3 medium beets, boiled in their skins, then peeled and cubed (at home)
Chicken stock (or melted snow) to moisten
Salt and pepper to taste (or mask it)

At home or on the road, mix all the ingredients well and form
into patties. Triple-wrap in foil, place on the engine, and hope for
company.

Baked Gilroy Garlic Highway 101

Gilroy, California, as the signs will tell you as you approach it on
Route 101, is the garlic capital of America. This is a good dish to
cook on your way to a date that will probably fizzle anyway. The pri-
mary purpose of the bread crumbs, by the way, is to act as a reservoir of oil for the cooking process.

3 heads of garlic (if you can find it, the so-called elephant garlic
　　is spectacular for this dish)
¹/₂ cup coarse fresh bread crumbs
French or Italian bread
California olive oil, preferably from a small grove that numbers its
　　pressings and buys its bottle graphics from artists waiting to get
　　their first wine-label contracts

1. At home, separate the cloves of garlic, but do not peel them.
Place the garlic and bread crumbs in separate bowls and cover with
oil, soaking them for 1 hour. Drain, then package about 10 cloves to
a serving, sprinkling liberally with the bread crumbs. (You can re-
cycle the oil for salad dressing.)

2. Place anywhere on the engine where there is a reasonable
amount of heat, and cook until the garlic is very soft. You may be
able to determine this without opening the packages; it should take
about 1 hour.

3. To eat, poot the garlic cloves out of their skins onto crusty
slices of French or Italian bread, or directly into your mouth.

Smart Car Salmon for Dummies

By now, we've all noticed that *smart* has become one of our
dopey era's favorite adjectives. Attractive people of both sexes are
constantly being referred to as "smart and funny." Sunday supple-
ment magazines tuck their relentlessly middlebrow recipes into a
department called "Eat Smart." There's a cereal called Smart Start,
and fake butter called Smart Balance. We've even seen a running
column somewhere titled "Think Smart," which is what we would
have thought was the alternative to not thinking at all.

We're reminded of a John Cheever story called "The Chaste Clarissa," in which a cad finally figures out how to seduce a woman idling away the summer in a resort town while her husband is away. She's not too bright, this lady, so the guy decides the way to break down her resistance is to flatter her over how smart she is. There's the lesson: the way into America's knickers, if you're selling something, is to congratulate it on its brilliance.

At the same time, oddly enough, there's been a tremendously successful line of how-to books based on the premise that we're all dumb. Evidently, we're of two minds about ourselves. We can be instructed to celebrate our stellar intelligence when buying breakfast cereal, but will freely accept moron status when we're standing in a bookstore aisle, intent on learning how to taste wine, auction stuff on the Internet, buy a house, learn English grammar . . . you name it.

Now we have a Smart Car. Not smart as in "smart bomb," of course—it doesn't home in on its destination all by itself—but smart as in, "You'd be a dope not to buy this car if you live in a place where it would be nice to be able to park nose-in to the street and still not have your rear end stick out into traffic." The little Daimler product will no doubt catch on in the cities, probably cutting into the Vespa market for people who aren't waterproof. And we'll know it has really arrived when bookstores start stocking a maintenance and repair manual called *Smart Cars for Dummies*.

Meanwhile, here's a recipe you can make on your Smart Car while heading for the Mensa meeting.

DISTANCE: 40–50 MILES, OR 3 BLOCKS IN THE IDEAL

SMART CAR ENVIRONMENT AT RUSH HOUR

1/2 pound salmon fillet, cut into 1-inch strips

1 small or 1/2 large yellow squash, cut into matchsticks

6 to 8 grape tomatoes, halved

1 large clove garlic, minced

3 tablespoons olive oil

Salt and pepper to taste

1. At home, toss the salmon, squash, tomatoes, and garlic together with the oil; add salt and pepper to taste. Marinate for 15 minutes. Divide the ingredients among 2 or 3 foil packages, moistening with a little more oil if necessary. Wrap.

2. Turn once during cooking, unless the packages are surrounded by two medium-hot engine surfaces. The dish is done when the salmon flakes easily.

Open Sesame Fillet (Sesame Sole Food)

Sesame, whether in seed or oil form, has a perfect California culinary résumé . . . it's a great "fusion" ingredient, lending instant international panache to whatever recipe you toss it into, *and* it's good for you. Its fats are unsaturated, it's got vitamin E, and it's a good source of protein. It departs from a lot of things that come out of California, though, in that it is quite stable, has a long shelf life, and isn't likely to go rancid.

Depending on just how Asian-fused you want your sole to be, you can take your pick of either light or dark sesame oil. The light stuff is made from raw seeds, while the dark is made from toasted sesame and is more commonly used in the mysterious East, which is due west of California. Very dis-Orienting: no wonder "Asian" became the proper thing to say.

DISTANCE: 50 MILES

1 pound sole fillets

³/₄ cup sesame oil

1 bunch small scallions, including half of the green parts, thinly sliced
¹/₄ cup sake
Salt and pepper (freshly ground green or pink peppercorns would be
ideal) to taste

At home, put the sole in a shallow bowl with the sesame oil and
let stand about 1 hour, turning carefully several times. Drain the sole
and divide into 4 portions on sheets of foil. Sprinkle with the scallions, sake, salt, and pepper. Wrap. Place on a medium-hot engine
surface and drive for about an hour.

Corvette Stingray

Skate, or ray, is a much-neglected food. We formerly speculated
that this was because people had seen too many underwater horror
films, but this leaves open the question of why squid is so wildly
popular—there are, after all, sixty-foot calamari out there, with eyes
like basketballs and beaks that could take off your arm.

A big advantage of skate is that since it is neglected, it's usually
cheap if you can find it. Since you will not find it frozen in a Kroger's
in the Midwest, it passes muster as a trendy California food.

As for Corvettes, we're aware that Chevy dropped the "Stingray"
nameplate some years ago, around the time it decided to price
twenty-two-year-old heavy-equipment operators out of their market and go after the Porsche demographic. But there is a rumor
going around that, just like *Manifold Destiny,* the old badge may
make a comeback—on a $100,000, 650-hp Vette.

Skate, which never crossed Chevy's mind as a naming option,
will still be cheap.

DISTANCE: 55–85 MILES

1 stick butter, plus extra for buttering foil

1 small red onion, chopped

1/4 cup capers, drained and minced (or rinsed and minced, if you're using the upscale kind packed in salt)

1 skate wing, cut into serving pieces

1. At home, melt the butter in a saucepan, add the onion and capers, and simmer over very low heat about 15 minutes. Place the pieces of skate on buttered foil, brush well with the onion-caper mixture, and wrap.

2. Cook 1 to 1½ hours on a medium-hot part of the engine, perhaps atop the injector housing. Be sure not to overcook, or you'll wind up with skate*board*, another California favorite.

Eats Fit for a Honda Fit

*N*oodling around on the Web recently, we came across a site titled "Low-Priced Fits." Having taken a few high-priced fits ourselves—five marriages' worth—we checked the site and came up with a swoopy little five-door Honda, a low-priced Fit indeed at just under fourteen grand. Needless to say, this is a car that requires a healthful recipe to tuck under the hood . . . something low-priced that will keep you fit.

Being healthy is as much a mental state as a physical one; while buying a car called the Fit might be a karmic boost, it's just a thoughtful beginning. A growing segment of Americans believes that a good diet will get you exactly nowhere if it's not backed by purity of thought and spirit. Being prime exponents of the "try anything" school of existence, we're perfectly willing to give this line of reasoning a chance, at least once anyway. If everyone would cook with this extended thoughtfulness, the health-care debate could be solved tomorrow.

Say you're driving your Fit (as opposed to having a fit while driving) around the coast of Oregon at the right time of year. Stop at the mouth of a river, wade in, and hand-net a salmon, glistening in the morning sun. When its spirit has departed this vale, slice fillets and put them on ice.

Toward lunchtime, pull off in a shady spot and forage for some wild chives (see Gibbons, Euell). Gather a few handfuls, rinse in the nearby sparkling stream, and cut off the roots. Cut an appropriate amount of a salmon fillet into sticks the thickness of a pencil.

Arrange a lovely layer of fish and vegetable, alternating colors, on a sheet of foil sparingly coated with extra virgin (for aren't we all pure of heart?) olive oil, sprinkling with a pinch of dulse (dried seaweed) flakes, and wrap snugly, being careful to leave the top and bottom of the packet smooth and free of seams. Do the second and third wrappings and find a safe place on the engine for your main course.

Now, as you pass through the next perfect little town, keep an eye peeled for the nearest cooperative bakery, ideally sited across from a village green full of lambs working as lawn mowers rather than playing a onetime walk-off role as innocent victims in corporate America's monstrous meat-o-rama. Buy a loaf of seven-grain bread, and try to avoid a hernia lugging it out to the Fit.

When it's time to dine, find a pleasant spot and check the fish; it should be a lovely pink, just past raw in the center, surrounded by fragrant juices. Array minicanvases of alternating chives and salmon on very thin seven-grain (you want to be able to chew the stuff) and sprinkle with liquids from the foil packet. Devour, neatly and politely, accompanied by a glass of pure-as-the-driven-snow meltwater from a mountain stream, purified by filtering through your own good thoughts.

So there you have it, a healthy lunch that strikes as many of the proper moral and spiritual bells and whistles as possible in one delightful and wholesome meal. Think lovely, think healthy, and those little *i*'s and *t*'s will be lining up at your doorstep, just waiting to be dotted and crossed.

Scion S'mores

Sometimes, marketing trips over the rug and funny things happen. Toyota learned this with its Scion, a small van/wooden-toy/cartoon-figure of a vehicle that was aimed at ironic hipsters, those cool enough to still be attached to Mom and Dad's purse strings as they bravely grew, or at least tried to grow, their first beards. Then they untucked their shirttails, got apartments in the big city, and decided that pretty much everything in the world was meant for them, and them only.

Before they could claim the Scion for their very own, though, an odd thing happened: oldsters started buying them. It seems that in coming up with the ultimate bare-bones "I'll Be Your Mirror" automobile, Toyota actually gave the world a rational small car, devoid of silly bells, meaningless options, and stupid car tricks, of features that sound good in the showroom but would be tossed away in the first couple of weeks of driving if they weren't paid for already.

For it was decently made, and cheap. As square as an ice cube, it had large windows and great visibility. Devoid of dumb tricks, there was room for easily read controls and switches; lacking sexy, sleek curves that served no purpose, the car was easy to enter and comfortable once you were in. The engine was big enough to get you there without picking up a string of summonses.

Older, stiffer owners didn't need hired help to get out at the end of the ride. Bags of groceries could be lifted from the rear without a doorman. With no apologies to the rarefied world of design, the thing worked, and the aging crowd bought it.

And what to munch on during a pleasant afternoon drive? A snack from the past, of course, to go with finally getting another chance at that beloved string of wooden toy cars you got for Christmas ages ago, when you were about five. We're deep in culinary dreamland here: time for some s'mores and a ride on the Sugarland Express.

DISTANCE: 40 MILES

For each s'more (warning, they are habit-forming):
  2 graham crackers (Since you're an adult now, any kind you wish—
    honey, plain . . .)
  1 marshmallow
  1 thin square chocolate, broken from an individual-sized bar, milk or
    semisweet, depending on how much of a child you wish to be
    today

1. Place 1 cracker on foil, then stack on top of it a marshmallow, a square of chocolate, and another cracker.

2. Wrap firmly, but be very careful not to crack the cracker. A smashed s'more is a dispiriting sight.

3. When wrapped three times, place in a warm, secure spot on the engine. We're attempting only to melt the marshmallow and chocolate, not grill a porterhouse steak.

4. Unwrap carefully, again avoiding crushing the crackers. Serve with a large stack of napkins.

The moral of the story, of course, is don't try to eat your ancestors' lunch before they've finished dessert. There's still time to cut you out of the will, kid.

4

International Car-Engine Cuisine

*G*lobalization is one of the watchwords of the new millennium. In our new global economy, we keep being told the world is flat—a mantra repeated about as often, nowadays, as "the world is fat."

In keeping with both trends, we're happy to offer a global take on car-engine cooking. We hope these recipes put you in the proper spirit of international cooperation, as part of the coalition of the filling. And don't forget, this technique is especially convenient if you get globalized out of a job, and wind up living in your car.

Nifty NAFTA Nachos

We would never think to question the fine, altruistic goals behind NAFTA—the North American Free Trade Agreement. To allow a brief moment of cynicism, though, the main beneficiaries seem to be outfits such as auto and apparel manufacturers that now get to use labor that is, to be polite, a tad less expensive than the going rate in the United States. We really haven't seen any stories about Canadian companies opening knit-hat plants in Bismarck, North Dakota, or Mexican entrepreneurs scouting factory space in Flint, Michigan, for their new widget assembly lines.

But enough of our silly caviling. In the spirit of free trade, we offer this treat.

Say you're parked, idling, on some dirt road just across the border from Chihuahua, Mexico (where they grow the little dogs), in the Sierra Vieja Mountains, about twenty miles north of where Texas Route 170 comes to a dead end at Candelaria. You're waiting for your own private free trade shipment, which might take the form of either warm bodies or something to make the body warmer. Given the vagaries of your international partners' schedule for crossing the Rio Grande, you might get a bit peckish. Here's the answer: toasty nachos.

The best part of this recipe is that you can avoid commercial chips and use freshly made tortillas, thus gainfully employing the local populace.

**DISTANCE: ABOUT 60 MILES, OR FOREVER,
DEPENDING ON THE PRESENCE OF *FEDERALES***

Lard
Four 8-inch corn tortillas
1 small can jalapeño peppers, thinly sliced
1/2 pound Monterey Jack cheese, or a good Cheddar, shredded

At home or on the road, grease 4 squares of foil with lard. With a sharp knife, score, but do not cut through, each tortilla. Place a tortilla on each foil square, then distribute the sliced peppers over all. Sprinkle with the cheese, and wrap tightly. Place on the hottest available spot on the engine and cook until crisp, 30 to 45 minutes. Unwrap, crack at the score marks, and chow down.

Depending on the size of your manifold and the length of your wait, we suggest eating each batch in succession, to pass the time and ensure freshness. Watch your back.

Bento Boxster

Recently, we took a fresh look at the Boxster, Porsche's lovely little roadster that got its name because of its "boxer" engine—a flat six, with the pistons "punching" back and forth on the horizontal. It's a great engine, with one funny quirk: you can't see it.

The Boxster's 2.7-liter, 245-hp engine (295 if you shell out for the 3.4-liter version) is accessible only to the highly trained mechanic at the Porsche dealer—did you think the boys in Zuffenhausen wanted *you* fooling around with their baby? Lift the hood and you'll see cargo space. Lift the trunk and you'll see the same, along with a sleek little dipstick sheath—they will grant you that level of competence. The Boxster makes nice noises, but you can't see where they're coming from.

In a way, this seems like an odd marketing miscalculation, depriving the American male car owner of the time-honored tradition of standing in front of an open hood, dreamily gazing at his new engine, watching the shiny clockworks jiggle nicely as the exhaust burbles away. Poke the throttle linkage and hear it go *vroom*. Man and boy are once more interchangeable.

As far as the subject at hand—lunch—goes, the Boxster is a disaster. Obviously, we're not going to suggest that you crawl under the car and blindly pack *kassler rippchen* up into any spot that will hold it, or maybe cram a couple of pounds of spaetzle into some mysterious cavity. But being bright boys, we found the solution.

DISTANCE: NEGLIGIBLE

1 bento box of sushi per occupant, purchased from your favorite sushi joint (If you own a Boxster, you'll have a favorite sushi joint.)

1. On a cool to cold day, put the bento box(es) into the front or rear trunk and drive like hell to someplace else.
2. Stop the car, retrieve the sushi, and eat it.

Don't try to eat while you're driving, lest you spill wasabi onto whichever optional leather surface you've selected for the seats. While desperately trying to clean the leather, you'll probably flip the thing, winding up with a bent Boxster and no lunch.

Bohnen Mit Wurst

One of us once coughed up $4,800 and bought a brand-new 1973 edition of the car whose initials you see above. That was back when owners of the perky, boxy little vehicles still flashed their headlights at each other, back when the marque had yet to achieve the status it garnered in the '80s, when each car came with a pair of yellow suspenders and a subscription to *Barron's*.

Since then, Bimmers have gone mainstream, and lost a lot of their quirky Teutonic cachet. So, in an attempt to bring them back to their ethnic roots, while simultaneously recognizing their thorough Americanization (hell, some of them are made in Alabama), we've come up with a crossover dish that combines German sausage (the wurst) with that old Yankee favorite, baked beans (*bohnen,* as they say in Munich). Our favorite supplier of bratwurst is the Haledon Pork Store, in Haledon, New Jersey, but you can use the supermarket variety (all the better for you if you live in Wisconsin) in a pinch. Just remember to make sure your wurst is good and fresh— you wouldn't ever want to associate BMWs with spoiled brats.

DISTANCE: 30–60 MILES

2 bratwursts
Butter for greasing foil
1 small can baked beans, preferably the molasses kind, not the ones
    made with tomato sauce

Split the bratwursts lengthwise and place them cut side down on buttered foil. Overlay with beans, being careful not to spoon in too much liquid. And, sure, throw in that chunk of pork fat they pack in with the beans. Wrap so the package is flat, and place on a hot spot with the wurst side down. Depending on the engine position, the brats should be cooked through and the beans well heated in 45 minutes to 1 hour.

Veal Rollatini Calabrese alla Passeggiata

Back in the early '90s, one of us got a dream assignment from *The Washington Post Magazine:* drive the entire coast of Italy, from France to what was then Yugoslavia. The trip took eighteen days, ran to 2,600 miles, and cost the *Post,* back when they still paid free-lancers' expenses, three million lire—the only time we've ever run up expenses in the millions of anything (in freelancers' *paradiso,* we get to spend three million *euros* on annual assignments to Italy).

The tenth day of driving found us in Reggio di Calabria, at the tip of the toe of the boot. From Reggio, you can look across the Straits of Messina at Sicily. We arrived at the city just as the early January darkness was falling, and found ourselves trying to inch down the main drag just as everyone in Reggio was turning out for the evening *passeggiata.* The *passeggiata* is an Italian tradition, especially in the small towns and cities down south. The idea is simple. The citizenry gets dressed up—and in Italy, this means more than just putting your baseball cap on forward instead of backward—and strolls along the main street. Not just the sidewalk, the street. It took us forty-five minutes to drive the six blocks to our hotel.

After we showered, turned up the lapels on our suit jackets, and put a fresh snap in the brim of the old Borsalino, we sauntered out to join the *passeggiata* ourselves. Our path eventually led to a place called Rodrigo's, where we enjoyed a starter of *linguine tramonti rossi,* tossed with cream, caviar, and smoked salmon, followed by *rollatini di Calabria*—veal rolls stuffed with pancetta, mozzarella, and lots of Calabria's signature seasoning, dried hot pepper. About halfway through this wonderful entrée, though, the thought oc-curred: we could have cooked the veal rolls on the engine of our two-liter Ford Sierra over the course of the six blocks we covered wedging our way through the *passeggiata,* and eaten at the hotel.

We'll stick with Rodrigo's, of course. But keep this in mind if there's a major traffic jam in your future, and a good Italian butcher is nearby.

DISTANCE: 75 MILES OR 6 BLOCKS

1/2 cup minced pancetta
Olive oil for greasing foil
2 thin veal scallops, lightly pounded
1/2 cup shredded mozzarella
1/2 teaspoon red pepper flakes
Salt and pepper to taste

At home, sauté the minced pancetta until translucent. Lightly oil a sheet of foil (olive oil, of course) and place the veal scallops on the foil alongside each other. Sprinkle each scallop with the pancetta, mozzarella, and seasonings. Roll tightly and wrap with the foil to hold the roll shape. Wrap in the additional two layers of foil and place on the engine.

NOTE: Wrap the rolls separately if engine space is limited.

CHRIS MAYNARD AND BILL SCHELLER

Toad in the Hole Under the Bonnet

One of us—if we may for the moment depart from the editorial "we" that makes us seem like Siamese twins—is an unabashed Anglophile, who drives his family nuts by playing Sir Edward Elgar's *Coronation Ode* at full volume during breakfast, and the other is actually part English. Both of us, however, can fully appreciate the nearly universal disdain that has been heaped upon English food. We're not talking about all the trendy eats available in the reinvented London that sprawls beneath that goofy Ferris wheel they put up; most of the capital's restaurants that make the travel pages serve foreign food, or some fusion trend of the moment. No, we're recalling the cellophane-wrapped Scotch eggs they serve in pubs, overcooked vegetables, mealy gray bangers—all the things that go to prove that the rest of the world didn't make up the English-food stereotype. Maybe it's just a matter of deeply ingrained bad taste: one of us once actually traveled through France—through *France*, for God's sake—with an English couple who packed along their own supply of axle-grease English margarine, lest they should have to eat some of the local butter.

And yet . . . and yet (strains of the *Coronation Ode* come up in the background) . . . the English larder, and the traditional English kitchen repertoire, have all the ingredients of a noble cuisine. Think of great joints of beef, rabbit pie, Devonshire clotted cream, steak and kidney pie, poached salmon, and well-hung grouse (no, not that kind of hung—go look it up in a game cookbook). Think of all the sweet and savory puddings, with the lordly plum pudding at the head of the lot (take it, Elgar). English cuisine at its best is the provender for a *Wind in the Willows* idyll, a cold, crisp night in Tolkien's shire, a calm-seas cruise with Aubrey and Maturin and a first-rate cook in the galley.

Then, of course, there are English cars. If the first really fine day of spring doesn't make you want to hop into a Morgan and take off across the downs and dales, you're as hopeless as a poorly hung grouse.

This is a recipe that calls for a deft touch, a little ingenuity, and proper care—rather like owning an old English car. We depart here from our otherwise ironclad caveat regarding loose, gooey stuff, but if you fashion a serviceable foil packet and have the right engine surface available, you should be able to pull this off—or see it through, as the English say.

DISTANCE: 60–75 MILES

1 egg
$\frac{1}{4}$ teaspoon salt
Pepper to taste
1 cup flour
1 cup milk
$\frac{1}{2}$ pound small pork sausages—breakfast sausages work nicely

1. At home, before assembling the ingredients, find a secure spot on a hot, flat part of the engine that will accommodate a sturdy foil packet. It's a good idea to do a dry run with an empty packet so that you know what you're getting into. To make the packet, start with 3 sheets of regular or 2 sheets of heavy-duty foil, placed atop each other. Bring the sides up and fold/seal the sides to make a little box or tray big enough to hold the batter, remembering that the batter will expand while cooking. Have ready another layer of foil sheets with which to make a lid.

2. Beat the egg with the salt and pepper, then slowly beat in the flour. Add the milk in a thin stream and beat the batter until creamy. Chill the batter for 1 hour. About 15 minutes before taking the batter out of the fridge, get the car running so it will start cooking right away, minimizing the time the batter remains liquid.

3. Poke the sausages with the tines of a sharp fork and fry until

lightly browned. Remove from the pan and arrange on the bottom of your foil packet, adding a tablespoon or so of the fat in the pan. Pour the batter over the sausages and crimp the lid onto the packet. Be careful when transporting to the car—you may want to fit the packet in first, then add the ingredients and crimp on the lid.

4. Drive through the countryside at a stately pace, popping open the bonnet from time to time and poking through the foil lid with a toothpick (*not* all the way through to the bottom of the packet) until a clean toothpick indicates that the time has come, Ratty and Mole, for your little picnic on the stream bank.

Jewel in the Crown Shrimp Curry, or, Ta-ta to All That

One of the biggest automotive stories of 2008 was Ford's sale of Jaguar to India's Tata Group, headed by legendary industrialist Ratan Tata. From Detroit to Mumbai, the air was thick with irony: a conglomerate in India, Britain's former "jewel in the crown," was snapping up the most British of marques. But Jags will still be made in England, and—who knows?—there may be a whole new Tata division devoted to maintaining tech-support call centers if the big cats revert to their earlier temperamental demeanor. We've come up with a celebratory recipe to mark Jaguar's passage into the hands of a firm born under the Raj.

DISTANCE: 30–60 MILES

6 medium shrimp, peeled and deveined (or more if you have the engine space, and increase the amounts of the other ingredients accordingly)

½ teaspoon garam masala (a spice mix available in Indian markets)

½ medium tomato, seeded and chopped

¼ teaspoon turmeric

⅛ teaspoon finely chopped fresh hot pepper, such as habañero

Pinch of salt

Olive oil for greasing foil

Combine all the ingredients and wrap in oiled foil. Place in a medium-hot spot on the engine. Turn the package once halfway through your drive. The shrimp are done when pink on the outside and firm throughout.

Wash down your dinner in appropriate fashion with a gin and tonic, or, if you're driving, a cup of Tetley tea. (Mr. Tata owns Tetley too.)

Curried Lentils Nano

Mr. Tata and his Tata Group have been busy with more than acquiring Jaguar. They've also just introduced the world's cheapest car, the Nano, a four-seat, two-cylinder model selling for only $2,500—a very touchable price. The idea is to give India a "people's car," and from what we know about previous "people's cars" (i.e., the Volkswagen), they tend not to stay home among their native people for long. Although Tata promises that the little buggy will meet European Union pollution standards, environmentalists are upset because it will put cars in the hands of people who hadn't been driving before. They fail to note that this will get the same people off their motorbikes, which generally don't meet the pollution standards of Stalingrad in 1958.

Anyway, we'd like to welcome the Nano into the world with a suitably humble recipe.

DISTANCE: 30–60 MILES

½ cup red lentils

1⅓ cups water

¾ cup cauliflower florets, cut into 1-inch pieces

½ medium tomato, seeded and chopped

¼ teaspoon finely chopped fresh hot pepper, such as habañero

¼ teaspoon ground cumin

½ teaspoon turmeric

¼ teaspoon ground coriander

⅛ teaspoon salt

1 to 2 tablespoons olive oil, plus extra for greasing foil

At home, bring the lentils and water to a boil; turn down the heat and simmer until the water is absorbed. For firmer lentils, use only 1 cup of water. Mix all the ingredients together and wrap in oiled foil. If packed loosely, the package can be shaped to conform to cooking surfaces on the engine. The curry is done when the cauliflower pieces are al dente.

No gin and tonic for you till you graduate to the Jag. Stick with the Tetley's.

Newfie Cod

In every country, there's a state or province they tell jokes about. In Italy, the people up north make fun of the Calabrians. In Germany, the Frisians are held up as risible clodhoppers. Americans have their rednecks, on whom the South no longer has a monopoly. And the Canadians love to make fun of Newfoundlanders.

Now, the people in Canada's easternmost province aren't all clueless hicks. From what we've seen of them, they're resourceful, hardworking, good-hearted folks with all the economic cards stacked against them—especially since the cod stocks have dried up, and we don't mean into *baccalà*. But Newfoundland is Canada's newest province, and the new kid gets the short end of the stick.

All this is by way of introducing our Newfie recipe with a Newfie joke—one that, of course, involves a car.

Seems a Newfie takes his girl out for a drive, and they end up parked at the end of a dock watching a big moon come up over Bonavista Bay. The guy puts his hand on the girl's knee and leaves it there for a long time.

"You know," she says, "you could go farther."

So the Newfie puts the car in gear, and drives off the end of the dock.

DISTANCE: 75 MILES

Butter for greasing foil
1 cod fillet, about 1 1/2 inches thick
1/2 small onion, sliced and separated into rings
2 tablespoons light cream
2 slices meaty bacon

At home or on the road, butter a sheet of foil well. Place the cod on the foil, and cover with the onion rings. Moisten with the cream, then lay the bacon strips over all. Wrap and place bacon side up on a hot part of the engine; turn when halfway done so the bacon side is down. The fish is done when it's firm and the bacon is crisp. (If the bacon doesn't get crisp and you don't like soft bacon, discard it and eat the fish—you've got the bacon flavor.)

A Tale of Two Livers

While a peaceful luncheon of sautéed foie gras certainly encourages lazy dawdling, to prolong the delight of an organ meat that simultaneously embodies "suave" and "lust," it is rapidly becoming an almost furtive pastime. That same band of public scolds who seem to insist that every kitten and puppy brought into the world be offered a free college education is now hot on the heels of the foie gras industry because of the way in which the foie becomes gras.

Which is to say: gavage, a time-honored process of feeding one's ducks and geese huge amounts of corn through a funnel or pipe to ensure a properly huge liver. Detractors say it's inhumane (as opposed to just lopping off their heads on an empty stomach), while farmers point out that the birds seem to like it, lining up for their frequent turns at the food nozzle. Incidentally, this is the origin of the phrase "getting your ducks in a row."

At the risk of sounding less than gracious, we'd like to point out that a quick look at the food court of any shopping mall will suggest that this is precisely how millions of Americans feed themselves every day, using plastic forks instead of funnels. Of course, no one is selling their livers for eighty dollars a pound, but that's a different debate. So far, they're not offering funnels at the food courts either.

Since foie gras comes from birds, we decided to take the hint and fly over to France for this meal, landing where the foie is still produced on small family farms. Recently Germany, Italy, and Israel have all banned production of foie gras, not that they were known for it. We're placing our bets on the French, who in this case have a good reason for their supposed contrariness: an inherited tradition of both taste and respect for many of the ancient ways.

France being France, we're providing two versions, for both the upper and lower classes. And now we proceed to the second question: on which stove shall we cook? In case you missed it, question one was whether it's wonderful enough to try on an engine. *Mais oui.*

Although France does not always spring to mind when thinking of epoch-defining feats of engineering, it's been fertile ground in the past. Think of Gustave Eiffel and his tower, of Fred Bartholdi and the Statue of Liberty. Think of Brigitte Bardot, all by herself (although Ms. Bardot is a committed animal rights activist, that's a different field of study).

For today's range tops, we've selected two models of Citroën, the first being the Traction Avant, made from 1934 to 1957, most popularly as a four-door sedan. They had rakish, high-striding front fenders, separated from the hood by free-standing bullet headlights. The cars were low enough to do without running boards for ease of entry, and, being front-wheel drive, had flat floors in both front and rear passenger compartments. They were greatly valued as taxis and limousines, and while there are reports of them being delivered in colors other than black, we've never seen one.

They were as distinctly French as a poodle wearing a beret and smoking a Gauloise. The front of the radiator grille was emblazoned with shiny dual chevrons, like a chrome corporal's shoulder. Late at night, on a darkened boulevard, they lurked instead of parked. If George Raft had run Marseilles instead of Chicago, he would have been sitting in a Traction Avant's backseat, his face showing a mixture of smirk and sneer through the shadows.

In most ways, the Citroën 2CV, manufactured from 1948 to 1990, was the polar opposite; both cars had four wheels, but that was about it. While the Traction Avant offered style and safety (an early engineering demonstration consisted of driving one off a cliff), the 2CV became known as the "Deux Chevaux," a workhorse resulting from a supposed early design mandate for "an umbrella on four wheels." The tiny things had a curb weight of roughly twelve hundred pounds and were powered, depending on age and model, by opposed two-cylinder engines ranging from 375 to 652 ccs.

The 2CV was a lot like the Ford Model T—a vehicle equally at home working on the farm or zipping into town for a new shovel or barrel of seed corn—but the Citroën was so tiny that it seemed like a large child's toy. The windows folded up and down as flaps, to save the weight of a cranking mechanism, and the roof was made of fabric, scrunching itself in pleats as it was pushed back. The seats resembled sturdy folding lawn chairs. The big difference between the car and a sardine can was that the car could hold a lot more sardines.

We hitched a ride in one on a French highway in 1969, and the charm of such a "to hell with the style demons" approach to automotive design quickly gave way to the sheer terror of riding so close to, well, just about everything. Of course, Citroën had the last laugh, for at that point it was exactly at the midpoint of its forty-two-year production run. As usual, the French were not concerned with our opinions, and they won.

And so it's time to eat. Pick your car and start your engine: lunch is coming up.

A Classy Lunch

DISTANCE: 80 KILOMETERS

1 dozen good-quality prunes, pitted
$^1/_2$ cup Armagnac
Butter for greasing foil
1 lobe fresh foie gras
Salt and pepper to taste
1 Citroën Traction Avant

1. The evening before preparing the meal, soak the prunes in the Armagnac, stirring gently from time to time. This is best done at home because the French also have DWI laws.

2. Smear butter generously on a rectangle of foil. Cut the liver in $^3/_8$-inch slices, salt and pepper to taste, and place on the foil with small spaces between the pieces. Wrap with foil three times, being sure to leave the top and bottom of the package smooth so that the liver slices will have good contact with the engine surfaces.

3. In a separate package, wrap the drained prunes in flat formation so the heat spreads easily.

4. Place both packets on the engine, giving the liver portion first dibs on the hottest parts, especially the large exhaust headers near the top of the engine. The object of the game is to sear and brown the flat surfaces of the liver slices.

5. Place the prunes in a secure spot where they will warm through by lunchtime.

6. Drive until cooked, ideally to that instant when the iridescent dark-brown-red of the liver turns to pink. If at all possible, stop to check it once, turning the packet over if necessary.

7. Pull over, open the packets, and serve on good white china plates. Eat slowly, and do not use a funnel.

A Déclassé Lunch

DISTANCE: 60 KILOMETERS

$^1/_2$ pound ($^1/_4$ kilo) cheapest liverwurst available (This may be a long
search, since a polyglot happy eater reports he's never heard
of a French word for liverwurst. Germany, y'know . . .)
Butter for greasing foil
1 Citroën 2CV
1 loaf Harry's bread
1 package dried prunes

1. Before prepping the food, check your car's engine. There won't be a lot of space, and if it's an older model, there will be even less. Cut appropriately shaped pieces of liverwurst from the master chunk and wrap them individually, the plan being to get as many packages loaded on as possible.

2. Butter pieces of foil and wrap.

3. Place on the engine and drive until heated through, or at least warmed up.

4. Serve on slices of Harry's American-style white bread, speaking of French engineering feats. It's an exact copy of Wonder Bread, a genetic match if bricks had genes.

5. Eat the prunes for dessert, straight out of the box.

Parting Thoughts

This third edition of *Manifold Destiny* finds driving, and eating, at a crossroads. Both activities have come into serious disrepute since we first set out from Schwartz's with our pound of smoked meat. A quarter pound would have been plenty for both of us, we're now told, and Montreal is a long way to drive for lunch. The scolds and Savanarolas are all around us: one guy recently wrote to *The New Yorker*, saying that elevators are a much more responsible mode of transportation than cars. Now, there's someone who has never woken up on a sunny morning and decided to go on a journey—unless, of course, he said to himself, "Boy, what a gorgeous day. I think I'll take a ride up to the thirtieth floor." We'll leave the ethical ponderings aside for the moment, and assume that hydrogen or plug-in electrics or some technology yet to be discovered will get us to Schwartz's, and that Schwartz will continue to be able to buy briskets from cows that have gotten first dibs on corn that might have otherwise been distilled into ethanol. We're a little nervous, of course, about whether car engines will continue to generate heat—

but meanwhile, we have to think about practical matters. Why have auto manufacturers decided that motors should look like sleek little portable vacuum cleaners, with fewer and fewer places to tuck in dinner? What will be the ramifications of the Zipcar rental phenomenon, where you can pick up and drop off rentals on the street, just by flashing your Zipcard at the windshield? Will you find the last person's leftovers on the engine? And will we ever turn on the Food Network and see an *Iron Chef* episode on wheels? ("Mario still has his fifth dish to plate, and he's almost in Los Angeles . . .")

This is too much to contemplate in this short space. But we are encouraged by an ad we saw, not too long ago, for the Dodge Journey. It showed a fanciful schematic of the vehicle's interior, laid out like an architect's rendering of an apartment. The front passenger area was labeled as a kitchen/pantry, and the driver's side was the den and dining room.

We didn't notice an elevator.

Recipe List by Region

The Northeast	Where to do prep work	Approximate distance/miles
So-Be Subie Spinach Paks	Home	40–50
Hyundai Halibut with Fennel	Home/Road	55–85
V8 Venison Cutlets	Road	30–50
Eggs-On Cheese Pie	Home/Road	55
Suburban Scalloped Scallops	Road	30–45
Pat's Provolone Porsche Potatoes	Home	55
Thruway Thighs	Home	50–200
Impressive Veal Impreza	Home	30–50
Down the Shore Cavatelli, Sausage, and Broccoli Rabe	Home	70
Safe-at-Any-Speed Stuffed Eggplant	Home	165–220
Speedy Spedini	Home	40
Stuffed Whole Fish	Home	140

The Midwest	Where to do prep work	Approximate distance/miles
Lead-Food Stuffed Cabbage	Home	55
Candy-Apple-Red Chicken	Home	85–110
Olds Soldiers Never Die Pepper Steak	Home	55
Hot Dog Surprise	Home/Road	40
Out-of-the-Fire, Onto-the-Engine Stew	Home/Road	85
Cruise-Control Pork Tenderloin	Home/Road	250
Any-City Chicken Wings	Home	140–200
Made with a 'Slade in the Shade	Home/Road	50
Milwaukee Memory *Mittagessen*	Home	60–75
Winnebago Welfare Wiggle	Home/Road	55–1,000
To Grandmother's House Road Turkey	Home	220

The South	Where to do prep work	Approximate distance/miles
Median Noche	Road	40–50
Good and Simple Cajun Shrimp/Crayfish	Home/Road	35
"Cajun" Shrimp	Home/Road	55
Orange Roughy Floribbean	Home	40
U.S. 17 Carolina Stuffed Crabs	Home	40–55
Pickup Ham Steak	Home	85
Maryland Crab Imperial	Home/Road	50
New Orleans Carpetbagger Steak	Home	30–50

California and the West	Where to do prep work	Approximate distance/miles
Ford F-150 Hot Texas Wieners	Home	30–50
Prius Pork	Home	60–75
Poached Fish Pontiac	Home/Road	40
Quail à la Veep	Road	See recipe
Donner Pass Red Flannel Hash	Home/Road	See recipe
Baked Gilroy Garlic Highway 101	Home	55
Smart Car Salmon for Dummies	Home	40–50
Open Sesame Fillet	Home	50
Corvette Stingray	Home	55–85
Eats Fit for a Honda Fit	Road	70
Scion S'mores	Road	40

International	Where to do prep work	Approximate distance/miles
Nifty NAFTA Nachos	Home/Road	60
Bento Boxster	N/A	Negligible
Bohnen Mit Wurst	Home/Road	30–60
Veal Rollatini Calabrese alla Passeggiata	Home	75
Toad in the Hole under the Bonnet	Home	60–75
Jewel in the Crown Shrimp Curry, or, Ta-ta to All That	Home/Road	30–60
Curried Lentils Nano	Home	30–60
Newfie Cod	Home/Road	75
A Classy Lunch	Home	80 km
A Déclassé Lunch	Road	60 km

ABOUT THE AUTHORS

CHRIS MAYNARD, cofounder of the YO-YO School of Art, lives in Warren, Rhode Island, across the street from a clam processing factory.

BILL SCHELLER is an intrepid travel writer and journalist, and has written or collaborated on thirty-five books, including *The Bad for You Cookbook* with Chris Maynard. He lives with his wife in northern Vermont.